WHEN
BOBBY
MET
CHRISTY

This book is dedicated to Ian, Martin and Brian.
Respectively, three young men who should still be with us.
Henry, Horgan and Santry. Bless you all. We miss you.

WHEN
BOBBY
MET
CHRISTY

THE STORY OF BOBBY BEASLEY
AND A WAYWARD HORSE

DECLAN COLLEY

The Collins Press

First Published in 2010 by
The Collins Press
West Link Park
Doughcloyne
Wilton
Cork

British Library Cataloguing in Publication Data

Colley, Declan.
  When Bobby met Christy : the story of Bobby
  Beasley and a wayward horse.
  1. Beasley, Bobby. 2. Jockeys--Ireland--Biography.
  3. Alcoholics--Ireland--Biography. 4. Captain
  Christy (Race horse)
  I. Title
  798.4'5'092–dc22

      ISBN-13: 9781848890398

Typesetting by The Collins Press
Typeset in Bembo 12 pt
Printed in Malta by Gutenberg Press Limited

Contents

Acknowledgements

This book would not have been possible without all those who believed it to be a good idea. Not least of these were Tom Taaffe and his sister, Olive Gallagher, who were supportive from the outset and had such incredible goodwill towards the project. Their memories of the time were as perceptive as they were sometimes painful. Olive's redoubtable contacts put me in touch with many people who were able to contribute greatly. Many thanks to them both. I am also grateful to Bobby's wives, Shirley and Linda, who were wonderful sources of insight into Bobby's hidden depths.

Thanks also to those who gave of their valuable time to recount stories and anecdotes – Jimmy Kelly, John Nicholson, Tos Taaffe, Ted Walsh, Tony O'Hehir, Austin Darragh, Richard Pitman, Pat Murphy, Linda Jewell, Willie Robinson, Claude Duval and many more, most of whom deserve a book in their own right.

Many thanks too to Pat Samuel who endured many hours of interrogation by phone from his base in New Zealand and who could not have been more forthcoming about his role in the story.

Indeed, to all those who in some way lent a hand, or whose encouragement was vital, my gratitude is unstinting.

Special mention must also go to all those at The Collins Press and to Aidan Power whose help and assistance (not to mention hard work) was a constant source of encouragement.

To my mother, Eithne Colley, and mother-in-law, May Downey: eternal thanks to a doughty pair for their constant and irrefutable faith.

And to Mairead, without whom ... well, without whom there would not be much to look forward to each day.

As for the rest of you – and you know who you are – who provided a network of forbearance, support and friendship from Crookhaven to Cork, to Dublin, Wexford, Kerry, New York, New Jersey, Seattle, Toronto and many points in between, my appreciation will be forever undimmed.

Prologue

As Pat Taaffe legged him up onto Captain Christy's broad bay back in the Cheltenham parade ring ahead of racing's greatest prize – the Grade 1 Cheltenham Gold Cup – Bobby Beasley looked out over the green sward of Prestbury Park. He reflected on his crazy life and he knew in the next fifteen minutes he would face either apogee or ignominy. He had long ago resolved that it would be the former. After everything he had been through, the latter was not an option.

Glancing around, he could see happy-chappy Terry Biddlecombe on the Queen's horse Game Spirit, characteristically chirruping away non-stop. Richard Pitman, on board the favourite, Pendil, looked dreadfully nervous as the weight of expectation – both public and personal – bore down on his young shoulders. Ron Barry on The Dikler, which had won the race the previous year, wore a mask of professional implacability, while Bob Davies had the mount on the 100/1 shot, High Ken. That horse was not considered by the experts to have the jumping talent necessary to complete the course and Bob was looking understandably apprehensive. Tommy Carberry's lean and angular frame was on the American-bred but Irish-trained Inkslinger, the fancy of many Irish racing pundits. The field was completed by the combination of Bill Smith and Charlie Potheen; the burly Smith did not look particularly confident he could challenge the more fancied runners.

But Bobby was not engaged with what was going on in anyone else's mind. He was focussed solely on the job at hand. And what a job. Here he was, a dry alcoholic on board a headstrong and wilful seven-year-old novice chaser whose sporadically brilliant form was punctuated with moments of madness that usually ended in tears. It was not a partnership that provoked huge confidence among gamblers or racing's insiders. Understandably. Even so, in the post-Arkle era, a time when the shadow of one of the greatest jumpers ever seen hung over a sport, Christy had been adopted as the spiritual and physical successor to that horse, particularly by the Irish racing public. They were intoxicated by a triumvirate of characters: Pat Taaffe, Arkle's feted jockey and now Christy's trainer; Bobby Beasley, reformed drunk and Christy's rider; and Christy himself, an unpredictable genius of a horse. The public was one thing, but those pundits who rarely allowed their hearts to overrule their heads smiled wistfully and thought to themselves 'it can't happen'. After all, they said, no novice had won the Gold Cup since Mont Tremblant twenty-two years before.

But Bobby, blessed with a clear head and unfuddled by drink, had formulated a plan with Pat Taaffe and he knew in his heart it was something they could see out. He had come too far down the road of redemption to let anything else happen.

Christy's often frail jumping was not in evidence throughout the race, but then Bobby was riding him differently from before, holding the horse up and not allowing his obstinate and often reckless charge to dictate to him how he would run the race. Bobby had regained an almost youthful strength – a strength which had been partly lost to him as a result of years of determinedly self-destructive behaviour – and he was the one in control. Seasoned observers noted as much as they scanned the action on the legendary Cheltenham turf. To some it was unbelievable that a previously crazed jockey and a wild novice jumper could put on such a show of controlled, accurate and disciplined jumping.

Inkslinger fell at the tenth fence, leaving only five contenders standing. Christy fiddled at the water jump, but got away with it.

The tempo of the race increased dramatically as the field took to the country for the final time – with just over a mile and a half to the winning post. This also increased the pressure on jockey and horse alike, with the smallest error now a potential disaster.

The jockeys shouted warnings, threats, curses and encouragement to each other over the overwhelming *tharrump* of twenty-four galloping hooves on the hallowed turf.

This was shaping up to be a terrifically exciting finish, especially for those watching at home on newly acquired colour television sets. The expected contenders were there: the English favourites Pendil and The Dikler were prominent, Christy was bang in contention (albeit held up), Game Spirit and Charlie Potheen were hanging in and, worryingly for those who predicted catastrophe for the horse, High Ken was leading.

And then, as the horses approached the third last fence, television viewers heard the controlled and measured timbre of the *éminence grise* of racing commentating, Peter O'Sullevan, go up a gear.

'High Ken leads and there we have Game Spirit on the inside, then Pendil, then The Dikler and then Captain Christy. Any one of these five can win the 1974 Gold Cup,' he told the rapt audience.

'They approach the third last. It's High Ken being pressed

by last year's winner The Dikler,' he intoned.

And then as the race unfolded dramatically, O'Sullevan shouted, 'High Ken has gone and Pendil's been brought down by High Ken, leaving The Dikler in the lead from Captain Christy.

'And Captain Christy is motoring just in behind him. Game Spirit and Terry Biddlecombe is in third. Charlie Potheen is way back in fourth and they are the only ones left in the Gold Cup. Dick Pitman is up on his feet all right; so is Bob Davies.

'And now coming to the second last fence in the Gold Cup, it is The Dikler being pressed by Captain Christy,' an excited O'Sullevan told an even more excited audience. 'The Dikler and Captain Christy land together; Game Spirit is back in third and Captain Christy is going the best. Captain Christy for Ireland and Bobby Beasley with Ron Barry and The Dikler on the far side. Captain Christy looks like he'll win it if he jumps it.'

The outcome of the 1974 Gold Cup was now dependent on a 38-year-old self-confessed alcoholic and a 7-year-old horse that was widely regarded as a talented but dodgy jumper.

A Family History and a Triple Crown

I f ever anyone was born into this world to be a racing jockey, it was Bobby Beasley. The Beasley clan were imbued with the racing gene and it was destined that Henry Robert Beasley would follow the pattern set by his predecessors.

By the late 1800s, four members of the Beasley clan had won Grand Nationals, while Bobby's grandfather won races over fences, hurdles and on the flat and rode his last winner when he was eighty-three. Bobby's father went to England shortly after the First World War and for many years was the stable jockey to the fabled Atty Persse and won the Two Thousand Guineas for the yard on Mr Jinks in 1929.

Although born on the Cromwell Road in London on 26 August 1935, Bobby was an Irishman through and through, but his relationship with his native land and with what he later called the 'Emerald Church' (the Roman Catholic Church in Ireland) was more often than not a difficult one. While he loved Ireland dearly, he would later blame many of the problems he encountered in his life on the attitudes that prevailed in the country, particularly with regard to sex and drink. He later also railed against the widespread 'anti-English' bias which was inculcated into children at school.

It is somewhat amusing therefore that it was a simple bird which Bobby would ultimately blame for the way his life turned out. That bird was an albino blackbird and it would, Bobby later recounted 'have a profound influence on my character'.

The story went that his great-grandfather was a Protestant who was being constantly pressurised by his Catholic wife and daughter to convert to Catholicism. On one such occasion he impishly told them that he would do so on the day he shot a white blackbird. This was something his family had to content themselves with and the man himself undoubtedly thought he was in the clear. However, he liked to take potshots at birds with the shotgun he kept in his bedroom and one day he shot a dove through his bathroom window. However, when the bird was recovered, it turned out to be a white blackbird and he could not renege on his promise to convert.

The bird was duly mounted and, much later, Bobby kept it at home throughout his life – all the while cursing it and the effect it had on him and his family. Bobby's widow, Linda, has it still. Whether or not the bird cursed Bobby's life or if it was his own singular ability to press the self-destruct button that had such a dramatic effect on his life is a moot point. But that Bobby himself believed it was the bird's damn fault is undisputed.

What is also undisputed is the fact that, despite being surrounded by horses throughout his childhood, he took little interest in them until he was fourteen and was persuaded by his visiting grandmother to immerse himself in the family tradition. He did and would go on to become one of the best jockeys of his own or any other era.

That the legendary jockey and trainer Fred Winter would later say of Bobby that it was his style, strength, horsemanship, intelligence, dedication and, above all, his intense will to win that made him as hard as any man to beat, says all you need to know about Bobby's skill in the saddle.

Blessed as he was with those talents, Bobby was not necessarily gifted with the same genius when it came to dealing with his human counterparts and, indeed, maybe it was the same dedication and will to win that estranged him to many people. There were many who marvelled at his horsemanship while being equally horrified by his personal manner. Certainly in his early career he didn't care much what people thought of him, but his was a very complex personality and that impacted on many of his relationships down the years.

Bobby Beasley wrote himself into racing legend by winning the Cheltenham Gold Cup on Roddy Owen in 1959, the Cheltenham Champion Hurdle in 1960 aboard Another Flash and the Grand National on Nicolaus Silver in 1961. Remarkably, he is one of only five men to have achieved this feat: the other four were Fred Winter, for whom Bobby would later ride; his old schoolmate Willie Robinson; and, more recently, another two Irishmen, Barry Geraghty and A. P. McCoy, who famously finally nailed the Grand National on his fifteenth attempt in April 2010. Bobby's achievement is unique, however, in that he achieved his in three successive years.

Bobby's Triple Crown

Roddy

Roddy Owen has been described as a 'quixotic' horse which was difficult to ride and well capable of dislodging his jockey at any moment. This made him, in character, much like Captain Christy and it also gives us an inkling as to why, twelve years later, Pat Taaffe chose Bobby to ride his wayward superstar.

Named after Major E. R. (Roddy) Owen DSO of The XXth The Lancashire Fusiliers who, amongst other things, was a former ADC to both the Viceroy of India and the Lord Lieutenant of Ireland and also won the Grand National in 1892 on board a beast called Father O'Flynn. That horse was owned by Lord Fingall who occasionally named his racehorses after Grand National winning jockeys and whose offspring would later play a large part in the rehabilitation of none other than Bobby himself.

Ironically, as it would transpire, Roddy Owen – the man – was prevented from winning his first Grand National in 1891 by Harry Beasley, who trained and rode Come Away to win that year. However, in a report called 'The Headless Horseman' in *The Irish Times* on Thursday 6 March 1958, John Welcome recounted the story of Roddy Owen and reported that trainer Richard Marsh gave Owen his first serious chance of winning the Aintree classic aboard Cloister in 1891. It was a decision Marsh regretted.

'In the long run from the last fence Harry Beasley was a length or two ahead but Cloister, full of running, was closing with him fast. Owen, for some reason best known to himself, decided to do the spectacular thing and tried to come through between Beasley and the rails. Beasley, quite rightly, refused to let him up. By the time Owen realised his mistake it was too late and he was beaten by a length.'

The report also says that if Marsh was upset at the result, Owen himself was peeved too and told the trainer that he intended to take Beasley out and fight him, to which Marsh drily responded, 'I don't think I should if I were you. You might be second again, you know.'

Even so, Owen lodged an objection, only to become the object of ridicule for every Irishman at the track who had backed Beasley – and apparently there were quite a number of them. A large crowd surrounded Owen and 'threatened to lynch him'.

Welcome reports that Owen put his back to the weighroom door and faced the mob, saying, 'All right. But wait until it's settled. Then I will fight every one of you, single-handed or the whole lot together!'

Owen won the National the following year on the unfancied Father O'Flynn, beating Cloister by twenty lengths and, once he'd achieved his ambition, he kept his promise to turn his back on the sport. He signed up for an external appointment with the British Army and was sent to Africa with the then Major General Herbert Kitchener. He was awarded his DSO as a result of his bravery in action there and the Owen Falls on the White Nile in Uganda were named after him. Unfortunately he died at just forty years of age after contracting cholera while on active service.

Lord Fingall came across the horse that would become Roddy Owen after a hunting accident saw another of his string, Tuft, having to be put down when he broke his leg in a pothole. In January 1954, the Lord, his vet, Louis Doyle from Navan, and his trainer, Danny Morgan, went to the Curragh to cast their eyes over several potential replacements, but found nothing suitable. They went on to Nolan's of Kilcullen, County Kildare, where they came across a four-year-old which had been broken and ridden but never tried on a racecourse. Danny Morgan, who had won a Gold Cup (on Morse Code in 1938) and two Champion Hurdles (Chenango in 1934 and National Spirit in 1947), sat up on the horse and was immediately thrown off. He bravely got back up again and this time stayed aboard. He liked the horse and, more importantly, so did Fingall. The horse was purchased and sent to Morgan's yard on the Curragh.

In an article that subsequently appeared in the *Meath Chronicle*, Lord Fingall's stable hand of over thirty-five years, Michael Power, recalled how Roddy Owen won on his first time out in the Leinster Handicap over 1-mile-6-furlongs on the flat at the Curragh when ridden by Jackie Power (no relation) at the very decent odds of 16/1.

He then competed variously in bumpers and hurdles with varying degrees of success before graduating to chasing and winning the 1958 Leopardstown Chase under H. R. Beasley. In that race he carried top weight and gave 8 lb to Mr What (trained by Pat Taaffe's father, Tom) who finished second. However, when Mr What went on to win that year's Grand National, the connections realised they might have something rather decent on their hands.

In that year's King George VI Chase at Kempton, Roddy Owen finished second to Lochroe ridden by Bunny Cox, an amateur rider. They were highly impressed with this performance and decided to aim the horse at the following year's Gold Cup.

There followed an extraordinary act of generosity on Bunny Cox's behalf, when he rang Lord Fingall before the Gold Cup and told him that Bobby should have the ride. This came after a disappointing performance at Leopardstown on Saturday 21 February 1959 when Cox had ridden the horse.

'He told Fingall that Bobby had no ride and should be up on Roddy Owen,' Power recounted. 'Fingall didn't want to change things, but Bunny persuaded him on the basis that the horse always went better for Bobby.'

So it was that Bobby lined up in the Lord's colours of white and green with white hooped sleeves and green cap for the 1959 Gold Cup on board Roddy Owen.

As the race developed it appeared that the Irish horse would not be able to match the leaders Linwell, Lochroe and Pas Seul as they turned for home, trailing them as he did by several lengths. But then, in a final-fence Gold Cup drama of which there have been so many over the years and which Bobby himself would experience fifteen years later, Pas Seul fell and hampered both Linwell and Lochroe.

Bobby, riding on the inside and away from all the trouble, was left with a clear path and took full advantage, riding Roddy Owen out to an unexpected three-length victory at 5/1.

The following day *The Irish Times* reported that it may have been that Bobby and Roddy Owen were lucky winners of the race, but its reporter still maintained that the horse 'had jumped better than he had in his recent efforts at home' and had finished full of running up the hill.

'Coming to the last jump Roddy Owen did not look like winning. Pas Seul was in front, but fell and hampered Linwell in his run. Lochroe was only in third on sufferance and after the melee Roddy Owen dashed through on the inside to win in spectacular fashion. If there had been no last fence mix-up, opinions are sharply divided as to who might have won. Beasley thinks he would still have scored no matter what happened, but in my opinion, Linwell was the unlucky horse of the race. Pas Seul was, I thought, beaten when he came down, but many people will disagree with me,' *The Irish Times* man opined.

Bobby and Roddy Owen were sent back to Cheltenham in 1960 to defend their title, but Pas Seul stood up this time around and won in impressive style with the reigning champion back in fourth.

Nevertheless, Bobby had already got something rather special out of the festival meeting as two days previously he had ridden Another Flash to victory in the Champion Hurdle.

'Flash'

Another Flash was bred in Mullingar with what has been described in some quarters as 'a rather plebeian pedigree' – something which again would resonate with Bobby at a later date when he came across Captain Christy. His sire, Roi d'Egypte, a full brother to 1942 Gold Cup winner Medoc II, had won the Cathcart Chase at Cheltenham but had a meagre stud fee of just £7. His dam, Cissie Gay, had changed hands on numerous occasions – on one, she was traded for no cost whatsoever – but was a half-sister to an Irish National winner and had also produced a useful chaser in Flashaway. In due course she would also produce two other good chasers in Flash Bulb and Super Flash.

For his part Another Flash came into the ownership of John Byrne who sent him to Paddy Sleator to be trained. Initially, Bobby was not sure about the horse, describing the barely sixteen-hands beast as 'a bit of a cob to look at' and while the horse was said to lack the scope needed to be a top hurdler, the jockey reckoned he 'possessed a tremendous natural spring'. The horse won all four of his starts in the 1958/9 season, as well as winning the Irish Cesarewitch, and there was a good degree of confidence among his connections that he could dethrone the reigning champion, the Ryan Price trained Fare Time in the 1960 renewal of the Cheltenham classic. His main rivals in the run-up to the race, besides Fare Time, were the flat-bred Albergo and the former Vincent O'Brien charge Saffron Tartan who was, by then, being trained by Don Butchers in Epsom.

The 1960 Champion Hurdle was run on Tuesday 8 March and festival goers were treated to a revamped Cheltenham: £125,000 had been spent on a rebuilt Tattersalls' grandstand and enlarging the members' enclosure, while another £10,000 had been spent putting a hardcore surface on those car parks and approaches that normally turned into paddy fields under the weight of the huge number of spectators and their vehicular transport in the English spring.

Based on his prior form – and despite the fact he had been beaten by a short head by Albergo in their final pre-festival encounter when he was not subjected to a hard race – Another Flash was sent off the 11/4 favourite. This was also partly due to the non-appearance of Fare Time who struck into himself while exercising just six days before the race.

On the day there was another injury scare, but this time it was about Bobby. The day before the big race he had been riding a horse called Dunnock, but the pair fell and the jockey was left in considerable pain from a bruised thigh.

All that was undoubtedly forgotten once the tapes went up in the Champion Hurdle and from the off it was Tokoroa and the 1958 winner Bandalore who made the running, with Beasley's mount handily placed in mid-division and under no pressure. Saffron Tartan was the backmarker in the early stages.

However, as they came around the final turn to race up Cheltenham's renowned hill to the finishing line, Albergo, Saffron Tartan, Laird O'Montrose and Another Flash were in line abreast. Reports of the race recount that all Bobby had to do was to shake up the favourite to ease him home ahead of Albergo (beaten by two lengths) and Saffron Tartan (three lengths – despite the fact that the horse swerved violently to the left on the run-in), in what was a record time for the race of three minutes fifty-five seconds.

The London *Times* reported the following day that the Irish horse won so decisively that 'he marked himself out as outstanding among present day hurdlers'. His subsequent history might not show that remark to be justified, but it certainly illustrated that the horse was as tough as nails and possessed of no little talent.

Bobby's future wife Shirley was in attendance at Cheltenham that day and she recalls something of a panic before the big race.

'I was at Cheltenham for Another Flash's victory and I remember there was a big scare before the race – the previous day, in fact, when Bobby had a fall from a horse called Dunnock in the first race of the festival and received a kick on the thigh for his troubles.

'The doctors were not as thorough back then as they are now and the only advice Bobby got after the kick was that the leg should be massaged all night to stop it from going solid. Of course, who had to do the massaging? I did. We set off the following morning, while Bobby was still a bit lame and sore. But he won the race and I suppose it was the adrenalin as much as anything that allowed him to do so because when he got off Another Flash, he could barely straighten his leg and could barely stand up on it.

'The victory was very pleasant and a short while afterwards he'd forgotten his pain, but it was just as well he did win because there had been very high expectations about the horse beforehand. He had to be held up until they jumped the last, because he only had the one burst of speed, but that's what Bobby did and any worries they had about the horse being too immature for the job were unfounded.'

Bobby also later disclosed that he had been asked to stop 'Flash' and had been offered what was then a huge sum of money to do so.

Shirley explains, 'We got married in the April after Another Flash won the Champion Hurdle in March 1960. There was a headline in one of the papers after that race to the effect that "Beasley comes home with the furniture". This had to do with the fact that after the victory, Bobby was quoted in the papers as saying "Another Flash was carrying a lot of overweight today

– furniture, carpets … the lot!" But he had received a strange phone call at home before the race when a stranger guaranteed him the massive sum of £6,000 if he would stop Another Flash in the race. He would be paid £3,000 beforehand and the remainder after the race, when he had done the deed. Bobby slammed down the phone on the unwanted caller.'

'There I was sweating to make £500 – enough to get married on – if I won the race,' Bobby himself remembered later – after Another Flash won the race. He also recalled the incident as being a salutary lesson in how great the temptation was for a jockey to become 'bent'. It was fairly easy, he mused, for a jockey to set himself up for life with great ease and very little risk.

It would not be the last time Bobby was targeted by gamblers.

Another Flash was unable to defend his title due to a leg injury incurred in what was reported at the time to be a 'rough contest' at Baldoyle. It was supposed to be his final appearance before going back to Cheltenham and on 1 March 1961 – just seven days before the race – connections announced he would not travel. The race was subsequently won by Ryan Price's Eborneezer, who never defended his title as he was sent to stud to become the first Champion Hurdler to stand at stud in the UK.

In 1962, however, Another Flash was back with a bang and was confidently expected – by both the public and his connections – to regain his title. The horse had been housed with Arthur Thomas at Warwick for the season – although still nominally trained by Paddy Sleator at Grangecon – and he won each of his five starts that season. These results meant that neither Sleator nor Thomas would countenance defeat in the Champion Hurdle.

He was sent off the 11/10 favourite and in a race where the

early stages were reported to be as 'uneventful as the finale was exciting' he joined Quelle Chance, Cantab and Fidus Achates to contest the lead at the last hurdle. The danger was not among these horses and, in fact, came from behind in the shape of Fulke Walwyn's Anzio, ridden by none other than Willie Robinson.

Full of running but blocked by a wall of horses in front of him, Robinson hoped for a gap. Anzio's chance came when Quelle Chance drifted slightly right at the last and the jockey – thanking the gods of fortune – shot his mount up the rail and on to a three-length victory. Another Flash finished third, some four and a half lengths behind the winner and a length and a half shy of Quelle Chance.

During the 1962/3 season, the race was won by the one-eyed Winning Fair, who was trained and owned by George Spencer, father of future champion flat jockey Jamie. Another Flash nearly died from a vicious bout of enteritis but recovered in time to come back to Cheltenham for a fourth time on 6 March 1964. This was the first – and only – time the race was run on a Friday after heavy snow delayed the festival meeting. In coming back as he did, he displayed the sort of hardiness and longevity that is so rare in modern hurdlers.

Again he was the pick of the bunch as far as the Irish were concerned and with Bobby retaining faith in the horse which had given him the title in 1960, the punters sent him off the 6/1 favourite. This was the longest-priced favourite in the history of the race and indicated just how open a contest it was.

Among the other fancied contenders was Sir Winston Churchill's Sun Hat who was unbeaten in four starts and, as a four-year-old, was in receipt of 10 lb from the likes of Another Flash and Salmon Spray, but a series of mistakes coming down the hill to the final turn cost him the race.

That left matters between Bobby's mount and Magic

Court, a reject from Noel Murless' flat yard which was trained by former jockey and vet Tommy Robson at Greystoke in the Lake District.

The two were inseparable at the last but Magic Court powered away up the hill and, despite veering left on the run to the finishing post, won comfortably by four lengths. Such was his waywardness up the hill that the stewards decided to consult their newly installed 'camera patrol' but ultimately they decided there was no reason to take further action.

Bobby, with his fierce competitive streak and dislike for losing, felt his horse should have been awarded the race, but there may have been a degree of sentiment attached to his view, as subsequent comments revealed. 'He [Another Flash] deserved a second title because he was a lot better than the record books say,' the jockey maintained. 'He was a lively character who'd see a bird you wouldn't of a morning. When "Flash" was retired, he kept jumping out of the paddock and had to be sent point-to-pointing. That shows you what kind of horse he was.'

The Great Grey

By the time the career of Another Flash was coming to a close, Bobby's story had moved on. In 1961 he completed racing's so-called Triple Crown with victory on board Fred Rimell's grey Nicolaus Silver in the Grand National. This capped off three years of unbridled success and massive popularity among the racing public.

Rimell had purchased the eight-year-old grey gelding as the top lot for 2,600 guineas at Goffs' November Sales at Ballsbridge on 23 November 1960 from Mr W. J. Hutchinson. The purchase had been made on behalf of Mr Charles Vaughan, a Rimell patron, and the following day *The Irish Times* reported that Nicolaus Silver was 'a winner on the flat, over hurdles and over fences when trained by the late Dan Kirwan' and that 'he had been corn fed out at grass all summer'. He was bought as a staying chaser with one eye on the Grand National.

Fred Rimell was a successful jockey before injury forced his early retirement and a switch into the training ranks. He won the race on board the gelding ESB in 1956, the year the Queen Mother's horse Devon Loch was ridden by Dick Francis (who would later go on to successfully pen nearly forty racing thrillers). The horse mysteriously collapsed on the run-in with victory a foregone conclusion, leaving Rimell and ESB in the lead.

Prior to the renewal of the great race in 1961 there might have been conflicting reports about how Bobby actually came to get the ride on the Rimell-trained Nicolaus Silver, but there is no doubt about his desire to win the race. 'My ambition is to win the Grand National and keep up the family tradition. My grandfather won it twice, my uncle three times and my father-in-law twice. In addition, my father was champion flat jockey of Eire [sic] twice. There is a lot to live up to, you know,' he told one interviewer beforehand.

In his book *Kings for a Day*, the late Aintree historian Reg Green maintains that Rimell fully appreciated all he had seen of the lanky young Irishman and had reached the 'astute conclusion that Bobby was tailor-made to partner his vibrant grey gelding Nicolaus Silver, the recent winner of the Kim Muir Memorial Chase at Cheltenham'.

He further asserts that, 'overjoyed at being given another chance to sample all the thrills his ancestors had known so well, the 25-year-old had no hesitation in accepting the ride'.

This does not at all match up with what Mercy Rimell (Fred's widow) told Jonathan Powell in a *Daily Mail* interview in 2007. Mercy had actually ridden the grey in most of his work while at the yard and she recalled rather a different story.

'When we bought him we were told by the great trainer Paddy Sleator that we had paid far too much money for a bad horse,' she maintained. 'Then our jockey, Bobby Beasley, wanted to switch to the favourite, Jonjo, who would be ridden by Pat Taaffe in the heel of the hunt. Fred wasn't having that.'

Bobby's wife, Shirley, recalls yet another version of events.

'Of course, Bobby won the Grand National on Nicolaus Silver, having been asked to ride the horse by Fred Rimell. That day he had been knocked out in a fall somewhere and he was in bed when the phone rang. It was Mercy Rimell on the line. I knew those people from my father's day and she wanted to know would Bobby ride their horse in the National. I told her that he was a little indisposed because he was only semi-conscious after a fall. As it transpired, Paddy Sleator had a horse called Clipador entered in the National and I was not sure if it would run. In any event, it did not run and Bobby was free to ride for the Rimells.

'There was also a situation where Nicolaus Silver did not like soft ground – he was a top-of-the-ground horse. It had been very wet in England and there was talk of Bobby being offered other horses, but he ultimately decided not to change horses and, of course, the ground came up right for the grey.'

One intriguing aspect of Nicolaus Silver's victory is that he was targeted by dopers before the great Aintree race that year. The Rimells' suspicions were roused when an attractive woman, who had been seen at a number of race meetings in the weeks prior to the race, came to visit the yard posing as an owner.

Canny Fred was suspicious of the woman and, because of this, he moved his National candidate to a box usually inhabited by another grey in his yard.

'So they did the wrong horse and Nicolaus Silver was

unharmed. We didn't say anything until after the race,' related Mercy years later. Similarly, Bobby would recall that the dopers got the wrong animal, which was just as well as whatever they administered to the horse caused it to lose all its hair.

But whatever the truth about which horse Bobby wanted to ride, he ended up on Nicolaus Silver in a race which featured many of the top chasers of the day. These included the previous year's winner Merryman II (Roddy Owen's old rival), another previous winner Mr What and OXO who had won in 1958. Wyndburgh and Badanlough were also among the punters' picks. The horse Bobby allegedly wanted to ride – Jonjo, trained by Joe Osborne – started as the 7/1 favourite with Pat Taaffe in the plate.

Curiously, there were also two Soviet horses entered in the race. Back in 1956 when ESB had so unexpectedly won the National, the race had been attended by one Georgi Malenkov, a Russian who was a guest of the then owner of Aintree, Mrs Mirabel Topham.

Malenkov, who obviously had considerable influence within the ruling Communist Party of the time, resolved to return to Aintree with Russian entrants and, in 1961, two of them, Reljef and Grifel, were duly entered and allotted top weight by the handicapper. Neither had any influence on the eventual outcome of the race, however: both horses fell and just one was remounted before eventually being pulled up.

As the horses lined up for the start there was something of a kerfuffle when Jimuru lashed out and kicked Merryman II on the quarters and it was initially feared that the previous year's winner might have to be withdrawn. But, after Gerry Scott dismounted and the horse was trotted up and down to ascertain his soundness, the field lined up again for the start.

At the business end of the race – and knowing that the

ground had come up just right for his horse on the day – Bobby settled his mount immediately the tapes went up, with his primary aim being to stay out of trouble and avoid any early fallers.

In what was Bobby's second ride in the race – he had completed the course on Sandy Jane II in 1957 – he was content to allow initial running to be made by Fair Winds. Fair Winds was closely followed by Fred Winter on Kilmore, while Wyndburgh, Mr What, Badanlough, Jonjo and Nicolaus Silver came next in close order.

Reg Green recounts how Bobby 'rode the race of his life' after the first circuit had been completed, 'gradually placing his mount into a challenging position'.

By now Merryman II had assumed the lead and Bobby followed him closely after Becher's Brook the second time around. Bobby later reported the horse had landed 'out on his head' due to the steepness of the drop on the landing side of the fence. 'From Valentine's Brook back to the racecourse this pair held command,' Green said, adding, 'taking the lead from the second last fence, Nicolaus Silver maintained his advantage to race clear and win by five lengths at a price of 28/1.'

Merryman II was second from O'Malley Point, Scottish Flight, Kilmore, Wyndburgh and Jonjo (who, Pat Taaffe later reported, had 'run out of gas' in the last half mile). Only fourteen horses of the thirty-five entered in the race managed to finish.

The following Monday, 27 March, *The Irish Times* reported the victory on its front page, reporting that it was the fifth time in the previous eighty-one years that the race had been won by a member of the Beasley family.

The story also reported that 'strangely enough few people in Naas, County Kildare, where Bobby Beasley lives at Coolgratton House, backed his winning mount'. It went on to say that most of the local people overlooked the local jockey and backed the local horse, Jonjo, who was trained nearby, instead.

An anonymous source is quoted as saying: 'Although everyone in Naas and County Kildare is delighted with Bobby Beasley's victory, we had most of our money on Jonjo, trained by Mr Joe Osborne, and we forgot about Nicolaus Silver.'

In its inside report of the Aintree victory, *The Irish Times* also noted that Bobby's father-in-law, legendary jockey Arthur Thompson, who had won the race twice (on Teal and Sheila's Cottage), had played a vital part in the win.

'Thompson gave him a "heart-to-heart" before the race, advising him of the best position to take up in the often vital first half mile and after the race Beasley was only too anxious to give a lot of the credit to his elated father-in-law,' the paper reported.

Bobby had now completed a remarkable triple crown in three successive years and was, without doubt, at the peak of his powers. He was a national celebrity in both Ireland and England and seemed destined for even further greatness.

Unfortunately, as time would tell, that would not be the case.

Bobby – A Downward Spiral

Bobby had hit the highest of highs in his sport, but was about to embroil himself in the sort of self-destruction which would see him trying to sell insurance policies, dressed in an ill-fitting suit and wearing shoes that leaked in the rain. His was a spectacular descent into the abyss, one which dismayed all around him, wrecked his marriage, confounded what few friends whose loyalty he could still depend on and shattered every belief Bobby had about himself and life in general. In particular, Bobby's troubled relationship with the Catholic Church raised some issues for him.

He explained that as a result of his Catholic upbringing, he became 'a slave' to his 'warped religious environment'. Bobby maintained his teenage years set a tone that would extend far into adulthood. He spoke of growing up with a 'twisted sort of morality'. He was shy of girls, even frightened of them. 'To think of them was sinful and wicked. So I seldom went out and any hopes of gaining confidence was rudely shaken at one of the first dances that I went to; I couldn't dance and was afraid to try. But somehow I summoned up courage and asked a girl to dance with me. I was going round thinking of how to put a few steps together, without kicking my partner on the shins and knocking her down, and I began to think that we were doing pretty well, when suddenly I received a sharp tap on the shoulder. It was a priest. "You are dancing immorally," he said. "I want to see six inches between." Of course, at that time I thought I had been doing something wrong. Now, years later, I realise that it was the priest, not I, who had the bad, sick, twisted mind.'

Having been schooled in the strict Catholic regime which was then in place at Killashee Convent School outside Naas, Bobby reckoned some of the rules later had a psychological effect on him. One such rule, which required the wearing of bathing trunks every time the pupils had a bath – on the basis that the angels might be shocked if they saw the students in the nude – illustrates his point.

He maintains he was so insecure, he ran away from the place at the age of just five. Incidents like his brother being made to wash his bed sheets after wetting his bed or being told, 'Get out of this Church. You are damned forever. Never come back again' upon confessing to masturbation when he was fourteen, shaped Bobby's 'narrow, puritanical outlook' as a child and it affected him for many years. He believed that he had a lot of religion drummed into him, but not much Christianity. This was the basis of his later hatred for the Catholic Church.

★

While it was accepted practice among jockeys that alcohol was part and parcel of their already tough lives, most used it as a simple panacea against the many pitfalls they faced on a daily basis or simply to fuel a good time. But with Bobby it became much more. It became the central facet of his life.

It has often been written that Bobby's first ever drink was

taken after victory on Sparkling Flame in the Galway Plate in 1960 and it was from this moment on that he sank into a sea of alcohol.

However, his first wife, Shirley, maintains that while he did indeed have his first drink after that Galway success, it was not really until much later that alcohol truly gripped Bobby in the vicious maw from which he found escape so difficult.

Shirley, then a 'vivacious and very attractive' woman, according to her husband, married Bobby Beasley after a very short courtship. Bobby had seen her at the races and – terminally shy – asked some of his weighroom colleagues to effect an introduction, which they did.

He recalls being immediately smitten, not only by her glamorous looks, but also by her outgoing and warm nature. The pair were married just twelve months after they met and *The Irish Times* of 26 April 1960 reported that 'Miss Shirley Thompson, who married the 24-year-old Irish jockey, Bobby Beasley, yesterday will start her honeymoon today watching her husband competing at Punchestown race meeting. The couple met exactly a year ago at a Naas race meeting when they were introduced by Frankie Carroll, a jockey.

Miss Thompson is the daughter of Mr Arthur Thompson, former leading British jockey, and Mrs Thompson, who now live at Kilcloran House, Camolin, County Wexford. Mr Thompson won the Grand National on Teal and Sheila's Cottage before retiring to train in this country.

'Bobby Beasley will compete at Punchestown today and tomorrow and Clonmel on Thursday.

'The ceremony, which took place at St Aidan's Church, Ferns, was conducted by the Rev. Michael Sinnott CC and the bride was given away by her father. She was attended by Mrs Eileen Bolger and Mr Frank Colben was the best man.

Afterwards Mr and Mrs Thompson held a reception at the Oulart Hotel, Courtown Harbour, County Wexford.'

And in an unusual turn of events, the man who drove Shirley to the church that day was none other than Nicky Rackard.

Bobby would later recall that his priorities at the time were far from what they should have been. After his Cheltenham Champion Hurdle victory on Another Flash he had returned to Grangecon 'to ride more winners and prepare for my wedding'. He was not joking about his priorities. 'I put it in that order advisedly. Racing was the only thing that really mattered – more important to me than the most important step in my life. Because racing *was* my life. I was only worried about how marriage would fit in with my work, what people in racing thought about me and what Paddy Sleator thought.'

Bobby would later reveal that Sleator – quite rightly – thought he was too young and immature to get married and implied that his jockey would probably lose his dedication and his nerve. He further showed his disapproval by refusing to go to the ceremony.

As Shirley Beasley now recalls, 'We actually got married the Monday before that year's Punchestown Festival. Bobby wanted to get married that day because Paddy Sleator thought that getting married would ruin his jockey. Paddy knew Bobby and knew exactly what he was like behind the façade he put on for the general public. He didn't want him to get married – he didn't like the idea of them being worried about "the wife in the stands". Bobby had to get married the day before Punchestown. It was the first year of the hurdle race track at Punchestown – I remember that. Bobby won one of the big races on the first day on a horse called Golden Era, Paddy's words to him were, "Well, at least you've done something in the last twenty-four hours. You've ridden two maidens!"'

She laughs at the memory. 'You get used to that sort of talk in racing, but Bobby was mad at him that night for having said it.'

There is no doubt that Bobby would later regret much of what happened during his marriage to Shirley, but his recollection of the wedding and its immediate aftermath can only lead one to wonder how the marriage lasted so long and, indeed, how Shirley ever agreed to marry him at all. Bobby himself admitted to being 'selfish and blind' for not being able to see how unfair it was to his bride that he was marrying her in the middle of the racing season and was not prepared to give her a honeymoon in which the couple might have learned something of the value of intimacy. He also berated himself as 'a husband who knew little about the facts of life and nothing about the emotional and sexual side of love and marriage'. He further said while that he supposed he understood the basic rudiments of his part in the act of love, there was a downside. 'In love, as in everything else, I was completely selfish. When I was finished, that was it. It was all over. I was certainly not deliberately cruel, but I was just as cruel as if I had done it on purpose, because I knew nothing about the mechanics. I had no idea how a woman should react or what pleasure she should get out of it. Shirley was a heroine, but we had got off to the most difficult start possible.'

In truth, if it was a difficult start, then the marriage as a whole would turn out to be a very challenging experience – for Shirley especially.

While there were obvious 'up' sides to being married to a top jockey – glamour, money and status – Shirley was to see more of the 'down' side of a jockey's life and especially so when Bobby really hit the bottle. But she was a very grounded person and Bobby was a very lucky man that such was the case. Her recollection of their wedding is typical.

'I never really thought anything about this being a glamour wedding,' she says, 'because I'd lived through my father's racing career. Even though Bobby had now won a Gold Cup and a Champion Hurdle, there were no silly ideas in my head about anything. I was marrying a jockey – plain and simple. There was nothing glamorous about our wedding; we had a very small wedding. It was not a high falutin' thing. We had made a decision on that beforehand, because if you start inviting people in racing, it becomes endless. So, the only people we really invited were the ones we socialised with. Paddy [Sleator] didn't come because he said he had to work the horses. Paddy actually very rarely spoke to me until after we got married. We were down in Killarney – in the Lake Hotel, I think it was called in those days – we were all sitting at this big table and there was a dance on and Paddy asked every woman at the table to dance, including me. From then on we never had a wrong word. I suppose it was just that, before then, he had never actually stopped to talk to me, or have a conversation. But we never had a bad word after that.'

Alcohol became a major feature in her life as it gripped her husband so completely. Unsurprisingly, she recalls that first drink with some clarity.

'He had his first drink after winning the Galway Plate in 1960, but there was no way at the time that I could have seen where it would lead. My father had never drunk before a race, but if there was celebrating to be done, it was done. I put him to bed on many an occasion. He could get well and truly plastered, but he might not drink then for a long time. If he was at a festival meeting, there was no question of drinking if he was riding the following day.

'But I remember Bobby that night and we'd had a pleasant dinner and, to be honest, I did not notice him drinking that much. But, the minute we got out into the fresh air, he went absolutely barmy and that was the first time I saw that. That was the first time I had to put him to bed.

'The reason for the celebration was that Sparkling Flame had last run somewhere down the country – it was an awful day – and he was beaten, but then he came to Galway having got into the Plate at a very light weight. He won by twenty-five lengths and the connections were called in to the stewards to explain the improvement. The thing about the horse was that when it was young it had an accident and broke a rib. They maintained that in the previous race the horse had a different saddle which affected his rib, but as Bobby had a lightweight saddle in Galway, there was no bother and this explained the improvement. At one point there was betting going on that both Paddy and Bobby would lose their licences. But the stewards accepted the story and they were OK. That's why the celebrations ensued.'

It was not, however, until the couple moved to England after Bobby was offered the job as first jockey to Fred Rimell that his battle with the bottle really began.

Shirley reckons that it was the dreadful winter of 1963 that kick-started Bobby as a full-blown alcoholic.

'We initially lived in Naas, but following the Grand National the year after we were married we moved to England. It worked out well initially and Bobby rode lots of winners. We lived in a lovely place near by Fred's yard and it was all very idyllic to begin with.

'But, I always thought that the trouble really started off in the winter of 1963 – the worst on record prior to the "big freeze" of early 2010 – when the racing was snowed off for months. There was absolutely no racing and he ended up going off with these various groups of lads and they seemed to spend their day patting him on the back, telling him everything would be all right and giving him more drink. I think that's really when he got himself into trouble. As I say, usually it would just be that they'd be celebrating something and that would be all right – that was just to start off with. But he did get a bit jarred during that six weeks and he did get awkward. But he was all right again after that for a while.'

As time went by, however, the situation deteriorated and Shirley was able to see what was really going on.

'Later on when things got worse, you might be out with someone having dinner and everything would be grand – no problem – but the minute he got to the car he couldn't say bad enough about the people we'd just been with. He was a very complex sort of person and he seemed to be trying to prove himself all the time. No matter how many winners he had, he always had something of a persecution complex. It was always "oh, they don't like me" or "they never give me any rides" or whatever. I don't know why that was because he was having plenty of success. He was very consistent and one thing I would never say anything against him was with regard to his talent. He was a bloody good jockey. But when you got him to the races, you'd have to psych him up – and coming home you'd have to analyse every jump. It was always a case of "did I ask him enough?" or whatever. He was always very critical of himself and of others,' Shirley recalls.

'When we first got married, all he wanted to do was to make some money for when he retired, which was fair enough. But when we got to England, he'd be asking me, "You know those people – why don't they ask me to ride?" I'd say to the owners or the trainers that Bobby was available and they'd ask him to ride and then he'd make up excuses as to why he couldn't. He just wanted to be asked. Don't ask me why – I don't understand.

'If my father got beaten on a horse, he just moved on. But

with Bobby when he was beaten it was a case of "I can never ride for those people again". I don't know why that was. He should have been confident in himself, but he wasn't. I could never understand all that attitude. When we went to England, the difference in attitude towards jockeys was unbelievable. At the time trainers in Ireland treated jockeys like they were boys in the yard. Over in England they were treated like little kings. I couldn't understand that and I couldn't understand why in Ireland when you won a race you only got the bare ten per cent of the prize money, but across the water if you won a race worth £200, you would probably get £50."

Even though he was hugely self-critical, Bobby still had his admirers. Richard Pitman was one of them and, as a young jockey, he felt there was a lot he could learn from Bobby.

'I remember him before he came over from Ireland full-time,' Pitman says. 'I recall him landing some huge gambles when he was riding for Arthur Thomas who was, of course, working in tandem with Paddy Sleator. The first thing that struck me then was how stylish he was. He rode quite long, but was still very, very stylish. He got into and down behind the horse to drive it forward. You see young riders and they look very pretty until push comes to shove and they start bumping up and down in the saddle and pushing down on the withers. Very few can grab them and push them so they elongate the horse's body, but Bobby could do that. He was brilliant at it because you could see him getting down in behind and making the horse extend. That was the thing that struck me about him. Also, in those days the riding was harder in Ireland so there was no quarter given by Irish jockeys and that was the case for Bobby too. If you went up the inside, you took your life in your hands. Bobby was riding for a gambling stable and they landed the gambles, but he was very, very stylish. Look at Nicolaus

Silver, for example. If you look at the photographs of that race, you can see that Bobby rode very deep and very long – there was an old saying in those days "the longer you ride, the longer you live" – whereas nowadays they're all riding with their toes in the irons and their knees over their heads.'

Former Champion jockey Terry Biddlecombe was another fan. 'There were many good sides to him and I loved the way he rode,' he says. 'He really was a good guy and the fact that he'd won all the main prizes showed just how good he was. Certainly, to become the Champion Jockey you have to win more often than he did, but when he was on the right horse, he really could do the trick. In the end he simply lost his way and when he did he was a different character. He went out on a limb, which was very sad. He was very isolated and the Jekyll and Hyde character in him did not help him in that isolation. And his problems were probably made worse by the fact that he wouldn't talk to people. He used to go around with dark glasses and a fag in his mouth. Character-wise, he was great fun when he was going well. But he was a wonderful jockey over a fence. He would never kick, like the boys do nowadays. He was a very good jockey but, having said that, he was an even better horseman than a jockey. He was greatly respected.'

On this point it is worth noting that while Bobby had friends in the weighroom, there were not very many of them and even those who knew his foibles and put up with them felt he was a strange fish. Terry Biddlecombe, who was then the number two jockey at Kinnersley, Worcestershire, provides a glimpse of how Bobby was.

'He had all sorts of problems and he'd had them for years. He used to sit there in the weighroom and was in his own little world. He'd say "best of luck to you" and all that sort of thing when you'd walk past, but he was very deep in thought beforehand because I think he was quite worried. He used to get into a bit of a shell. You couldn't take the piss out of him because he didn't like that. I knew him pretty well and he was always fairly wrapped up in himself. Sure, he'd had his problems, but then lots more do in racing.'

Biddlecombe was almost unique in the weighroom though, as he was one of the few who could successfully wind Bobby up. On one occasion, they were at a party together and Shirley was with Bobby. Biddlecombe, characteristically, had noted that she 'was absolutely charming and was a very beautiful girl'.

'Bobby saw me looking at her one day and said to me, "You fancy her, don't you?" I said, "Yes, of course I do and if you don't want her, I'll have her." He didn't like that. She was a very pretty girl. Bobby had a short fuse and you could use that to your advantage sometimes – just to get him going.'

Even earlier in his career, however, Bobby had ridden against many top Irish jockeys and Tos Taaffe (brother of Pat who would eventually train Captain Christy) was one of them. He was not exactly enamoured of his young rival or of the tactics that he and Paddy Sleator adopted.

'Riding against him, he was not a nice rider. I rode against him many times and I often found him riding horses on which he could easily have beaten everything in the field, but he only ever wanted to win by half a length. You'd know in your heart and soul that he'd have a stone in hand and you'd be wanting to say to him, "Would you ever go on the hell out of it?" There was one day at Clonmel I remember I hit his horse and it went on to win by five or ten lengths and he got very bad about it.'

Bobby did, indeed, get angry about the incident, but Tos refused to apologise or show contrition in any way. 'Go away out of that,' he told the fuming winner, 'you're only trying to make a fool out of me.'

'Riding with Bobby, you never knew what he was at. Any legendary status that was bestowed on him by the press would probably not have been endorsed by his colleagues in the weighroom. There is no doubting that he was a very good jockey, but he was an odd bastard. He was an excellent jockey, but he had no personality and he was always on his own in the weighroom. When he was riding for Paddy Sleator, the two of them were well met. They were always trying to get the horses handicapped. Bobby Coonan also rode for Sleator and he was a bit the same. He was another very fine jockey but he was a bit of a character and the handicapper was always keeping an eye on what they were up to, especially as everyone always knew the horses could win easy. I don't know what it was about Paddy Sleator, but he must have had it drilled into the jockeys to only win by as short a distance as possible.

'There was another day at Listowel when I stopped Bobby coming up my inside – on another horse of Sleator's – and he was cribbing like mad afterwards. He could have won by forty lengths, but he had to go around the outside and he was mad at that. Paddy Sleator came into the weighroom afterwards and verbally attacked me. I told him Bobby had no right to try what he did, especially as he had so much in hand. I wasn't the only one who saw what was going on – the handicapper did too. Sleator was a great trainer, but he obviously had it drilled into the jockeys that this was the way he wanted things done.'

Willie Robinson was a childhood acquaintance of Bobby's and the two of them even schooled together at the Killashee school in County Kildare. Like Bobby, Willie was a member of the exclusive 'Triple Crown Club' having won the Grand National, the Gold Cup and the Champion Hurdle. He reckons that Bobby had personality troubles even then, although he witnessed this to better effect when the pair was riding against each other.

'Bobby was a complex character, but the one thing that really drove him mad was seeing other jockeys winning on horses he felt were his rides. He'd rather see you fall on one of those horses than win. It was not just me, it was anyone,' Robinson says, adding, 'he would have been more of a brilliant jockey and would have been champion jockey had his attitude been better. His attitude towards you would always have been unpleasant. If you made any comment to him in the weighroom all you'd get is a dirty glare. It didn't matter if you were praising him or criticising him. The result was always the same.'

Ted Walsh, television pundit and a Grand National winning trainer, is even more pointed in his view of Bobby's personality.

'I believe he was an awkward character when he was young, but he was all right later on in life. He was a jockey and he never worked as such in the normal way that young fellas have to establish themselves in a yard; he'd get on the horse and, when he was finished, walk away. Sure, he was reared to become what he became, but he was awkward. He did not have a common touch and he was not reared that way either. He was a jockey and he turned up in his jodhpurs and boots and rode the horses and then went home. That era is gone. That was there in the '40s, '50s and early '60s. But it is gone. You had to muck in with the rest of the lads and he never did that.

'Consequently he was seen as arrogant – very arrogant – and he didn't give a shit what people thought. If you were getting on a plane and you were told that there were free seats beside Pat Taaffe and Bobby Beasley, you'd sit beside Pat. Bobby was very intense – a bit like Richard Dunwoody in later times – and was completely driven. He was completely into himself. There was only one person in Beasley's life: Beasley. He was full of himself and while he mellowed in later years, at the height of his career he had a reputation for being awkward,' says Ted.

Observing from the sidelines, journalist and commentator Tony O'Hehir also believes that, in his heyday, Bobby was a bit of a pain.

'He could be a very odd character; if you did anything on him, or if he thought you'd done something on him, it was quite possible he wouldn't speak to you for months. Everyone will tell you that he was undoubtedly a great jockey – one of the very best – but he was a strange guy and was the president of his own fan club at times. He certainly thought he was a cut above everyone else as a jockey and that didn't sit easily with a lot of people,' he says.

Bobby was certainly a driven man and his focus was solely on winning races – something at which he was very good. And, in the racing game, not too many care what sort of a person you are as long as you are doing the business at the sharp end of the races. To do that, however, he had to be resilient on the course and Richard Pitman provides a good example of just how tough Bobby could be.

'The Irish jockeys who came over here were a tough bunch and Bobby was no exception. There was none of this "after you, Claude, there's plenty of room up the inside",' he recalls.

'Years ago there was a jockey called Joe Guest and he was known in the weighroom as "the Iron Man" and around Fontwell Park he was king and no one ever went up his inside. It is a figure-of-eight course and going down the hill they go like the clappers and Joe tried to go down Bobby's inner one day and he ended up going out through the rails. I can't remember if Bobby won – he probably did – but I arrived back to the weighroom sweating, annoyed at not having run very well and when I came in the door I saw Joe Guest with a big oak chair over his head and Bobby on the floor. Joe was just about to crash it down on him and, although I was very wet –

I'd never been in a fight in my life – I said to him, "Joe, Joe, put that down. It will only end up in tears for us all." He turned and looked at me and said, "Do you want it? One of the two of you is going to get this." Thankfully the stewards arrived in and it was all diffused.

'Those sort of incidents don't happen a lot, but it is amazing when you think what a physical sport it is, what with the falls, the wasting, the travelling and all the attendant pressures, I am amazed this sort of thing doesn't erupt more. On that occasion the Iron Man thought he was king around his track and he could go where he wanted, but Bobby said "no, you don't" and it all blew up.'

If Bobby was notorious in the weighroom, he was also gaining a considerable reputation in England as a result of a plan hatched by his old mentor Paddy Sleator. The Irish trainer was frustrated by the lack of opportunities for his horses in Ireland and even more frustrated that, because the bookies were so well tuned in to his abilities, he and his owners were never able to back his horses at prices which they thought were satisfactory.

Sleator duly hatched a plan whereby he engaged the services of a small – but larger-than-life – English trainer, Arthur Thomas, who was based near Warwick in the midlands. As a result, horses prepared and trained by Sleator at Grangecon in County Wicklow were sent to England where they were nominally sent out from Thomas' yard. Thomas had nothing to do with the horses at all, apart from the fact they were entered with him listed as the trainer. They usually won.

Terry Biddlecombe illustrates how the Sleator/Beasley combination worked. 'I used to ride some of Sleator's horses as well and it was obvious to me that the two of them had a combined genius. Not only had Paddy a genius for training them, but Bobby had a genius for riding them. They used to set the f★★★★★s up, didn't they? Arthur took the credit for training them, but it was Paddy who trained them. He used to win races by only half a length and as a consequence nobody really knew how good the horses were. Bobby had this very good wrist action and when he'd draw up beside you and his horse was still on the bridle, you really knew you were goosed then.'

Tony O'Hehir remembers this time and discussed it with Bobby years later.

'I met him a couple of years ago at Leopardstown, very early before racing, outside the weighroom. He was just back in Ireland and decided to go racing. He was looking very well and he was telling stories about the days when Sleator had the arrangement with Arthur Thomas to base horses in England. There were all sorts of yarns about how Bobby would be riding something at Warwick, say, on a Monday but would have had no instructions about what sort of horse it was or how to ride it. And, as the horses were on their way to the start, then Sleator would appear from behind a tree, or something, to give Bobby his instructions. When that happened, obviously the money was down and Bobby was expected to win; he usually did,' O'Hehir says.

Bobby was, of course, happy with this arrangement, but he got himself into a terrible state because of what he perceived to be a conflict of interest between what he was doing for Sleator and his official job as number one jockey to Fred Rimell. He had, he maintained, convinced himself that Fred and Mercy Rimell resented the Sleator association. Befuddled by drink or simply incapable of weighing up the options before him, he decided that he could not keep on the two jobs and then went and told Rimell that he was giving up the job as his retained rider. He told the trainer he was moving to Leamington to be closer to Arthur Thomas' operation. This was despite the fact that Fred told him he was getting some good young horses which he felt would do well in the long term. Bobby would not listen and Terry Biddlecombe stepped into his shoes as the first jockey at Kinnersley and would become Champion Jockey three years later. It was a massive mistake and one which Bobby would bitterly regret.

This was particularly so as the British racing authorities had been unhappy for some time with what Sleator was doing in tandem with Thomas and they decided to act. They banned Sleator's horses from running under the Arthur Thomas banner and suddenly Bobby found himself with no rides. It was an abyss. Having had two of the best jobs in the business, he was left with nothing and had to scratch around picking up mounts wherever he could. For a man who was now firmly in the grip of the drink, it was not a good place to be. This was a man whose fragile temperament was already under pressure.

'Nothing much was happening now,' he would later recall. 'The good days were over. My rides were few and far between. If it hadn't been for Sleator, I could have ridden for a lot of trainers but, by then, they had other jockeys. I'd lost my contacts, my main job and, as I discovered, my dedication too. Sleator had another jockey in Ireland riding my good horses. I was neither one thing nor the other. I was in limbo.'

The result, sadly, was predictable. While Bobby went to race meetings in the hope of picking up spare rides, he invariably gravitated towards the bar. 'I threw myself heart and soul into the gas life with its night clubs, booze and birds. My weight was getting tricky and I was nothing like as fit as I used to be,' he said of the time.

This lifestyle led to another major problem for Bobby. To counteract the effect alcohol was having on his system, he had to take so-called 'piss pills' – devastating Saluric pills which dried him out while counteracting his drinking.

As a contemporary, Richard Pitman was very well aware of what jockeys did to maintain their weight levels and he illustrates the mood of the time with a story involving himself and some gentry.

'I remember on one occasion when [Lord] Oaksey [formerly the distinguished amateur John Lawrence] rang me about this doctor he'd heard of, who was working miracles with people's weight, but he wouldn't go to see him on his own and asked if I'd come along. I forget the doctor's name, but he was struck off since then. Anyway, we arrived at his rooms and the place was packed with fashion models – each one more skinny than the next. In any event, the two of us were called in together – he must have thought we were gay – and we explained our situation. The doctor says immediately, "Oh, I've got the cure for you. Undo your belts, drop your trousers and touch your toes." We did as we were told and the next thing he jabbed us both in the buttocks with a hypodermic. "Just something to get you going," the doctor said. It was a diuretic and the two of us were peeing non-stop for days after it. Then he gave us both a huge phial of pills and sent us on our way. After a few days I was completely loopy – out of my tree. After a while my wife Jenny said to me that I was acting very strange and wasn't myself at all. It turned out the doctor had given us amphetamines and we were as high as kites, happy as sand boys and, of course, we didn't want to eat.

'In those days too they had just introduced a drug called Lasix – at the time the only diuretic you could get was called modiuretic and it was very moderate, it would hardly make your eyes water – and it certainly was the business. The first time I took one I remember I was due to ride at ten stone in Nottingham and there was no way I could do the weight. I got a Lasix tablet and by the time I got to Nottingham – having had to stop to pee every few miles – I'd lost eleven pounds in water from my body. Imagine what that would do to you; the first thing was that you got cramps in all your extremities – shoulders, elbows, hips, knees, ankles and so on – and the other thing was that you could not hear yourself speak with the booming that was going on in your ears. Those pills were absolutely lethal and, of course, they were outlawed fairly quickly. Nowadays, any simple drug test would show them up, but they were dangerous because, not only were you a danger to yourself, but also to everyone else. So that was an era of sheer madness.'

Shirley recalls that the newspapers even got wind of the fact the jockeys were taking drugs to keep their weight down and *The People* wrote that Bobby was taking ten 'piddling pills' a day, but she says this was a ridiculous claim, especially as he would not physically have managed to do so. 'If he took two or three it was as much as he could manage. The newspapers love to exaggerate,' she says. Even if they did, the truth was that Bobby was taking all manner of pharmaceuticals which were far from good for him.

Bobby was still racing, however and, having been offered a job by Derek Ancil to ride his small string, he got the leg-up on a horse called Post Mark in a Three-Year-Old maiden hurdle at Nottingham. The horse fell at the fourth fence and Bobby got a desperate kicking as the rest of the field trampled him. He was taken to Nottingham General where it was ascertained that he'd lost most of his teeth, his lower gum was badly mangled and his bottom lip was split all the way down to his chin. He required sixty stitches and was badly disfigured. On the morning after he was operated on, he took one look at himself and promptly asked a nurse for a gun so he could shoot himself.

Remarkably, he was back riding two weeks later, even

though he was still so badly cut up that many people did not recognise him.

But, because he was riding so infrequently, he was drinking a lot more and taking more pills. 'Even though I was eating little – for four months after my Nottingham fall I couldn't chew and Shirley sieved all my food – the alcohol and inactivity sent my weight soaring,' he said.

He had discovered, though, that even after a night on the tiles, the pills would take 5 or 6 lb of weight off him. But the effects were awful and when he was riding, Bobby found that his hands locked up and he'd get desperate cramps in his legs and feet and after a race he would be quite distressed. In fact, there was one incident at Kempton where Bobby was so bad after one race that Terry Biddlecombe – recognising exactly what was wrong – forced Bobby to drink a glass of water with loads of salt in it to try and revive him. Bobby sought medical advice and was told that if he continued the way he was going he would be dead within two years.

He had started on Saluric pills and then, finding them not to be strong enough, he switched to Hydra–saluric and finally to Lasix, which he said was 'the most powerful of them all'. He had no problem getting the drugs – on which, he later admitted, he was soon dependent. But there was little chance of him taking the medical advice he was offered.

Between the drink and the 'piss pills' the situation at home was becoming intolerable for Shirley. Bobby admitted being 'disgusted with himself' for falling so far from what he had been when they got married. But he was delusional as well and while Shirley was booking his rides and was 'a tremendous help, always covering up for me', he was still taking his self-inflicted problems out on her.

★

As far as his career went, oddly, there was potential redemption at hand. Fred Winter, now the master of the Uplands yard in Lambourn in Berkshire, offered Bobby the job as stable jockey for the 1968/9 season. Many counselled the trainer against such a move, but he was convinced – like Pat Taaffe would later be – that Bobby's latent talent would shine through. He nevertheless put Bobby on a probationary period until Christmas of that year.

He would later admit that – as things developed – he never knew about the full scale of Bobby's problems, but Willie Robinson, for one, was mystified by this. 'Fred Winter complained that he was the last person to know about Bobby's troubles, which is a surprise because in a place like Lambourn it is very difficult to hide something like that,' he says.

Initially the couple were delighted to put their sorry spell at Leamington behind them and the move to Lambourn was welcomed. That would not be the case for long.

Reflecting years later that the village was 'a lethal place for a heavy drinker' and that if he had known the place better he would have 'avoided it like the plague', Bobby persuaded himself that he would be able to keep off the gargle.

He thoroughly enjoyed getting up every morning to ride out at Uplands, getting to know Fred's increasingly accomplished string as he schooled and galloped them on Mann Down. The winners were coming too and although Winter was usually seen .as a slow starter, Bobby started clocking up the winners. Everything was going swimmingly until 29 November at Newbury when he took a crashing fall off the novice chaser Latour and broke his wrist. He hit the drink straight away and kept at it through Christmas – ruining the family's Christmas

Day celebrations in the process and greatly upsetting Shirley and the children. He maintained later on that he wanted Shirley's love and affection more than ever, but at the same time knew he was driving a wedge between them and creating an unbridgeable gap in their marriage.

Shirley remembers the time in Lambourn as being desperately unhappy and not at all what she had hoped for after the nightmare in Leamington.

'The year with Fred Winter was the worst of the lot,' she says. 'We were in Lambourn and Bobby's drinking was completely out of control. He'd start off on cheap stuff like sherry – cooking sherry. And then when he was not racing he'd be drinking Martini or Dubonnet and then at night time it would be vodka or gin. Bobby's aunt [film star] Valerie Hobson was married to Jack Profumo [the Conservative minister who was involved in a highly publicised sex scandal in 1963] and she got on to me to see what could be done with Bobby and to try and get him to go to Alcoholics Anonymous. She lived at Harrow on the Hill and knew this man who had treated all sorts of actors, so Bobby went to stay with him for two or three days. But it was always the same – he'd be off it for two or three days and then he'd be back on it again.'

It was a vicious cycle and Bobby and Shirley were locked into it. The slippery slope Bobby was already on suddenly turned into a precipice. He hurtled over it and so did Shirley, caught as she was on the wrong end of Bobby's rapidly changing moods.

Others were aware of her parlous situation, including Elaine Mellor, the wife of legendary jockey and trainer Stan (the first jockey to ride 1,000 National Hunt winners). Both Elaine and Stan were very good friends with Shirley. Elaine came to her and said that while she didn't want to interfere, she wanted her to know that if ever she was in trouble she could come to them.

Being responsible for two small children at this point – as well as trying to mind Bobby as best she could – it was good to know she had an escape route. She would soon need it, after an incident at the wedding of Bobby's weighroom colleague Josh Gifford.

'After Josh Gifford's wedding, the whole thing started to go pear-shaped. He went completely berserk,' Shirley relates ruefully. 'We were up somewhere near Banbury where Josh got married, although we were living in Lambourn which was quite a distance away. After the wedding we went off with a load of people and Bobby was having a whale of a time. After a while I remember thinking "how the hell am I going to get home?" He would not let me drive and insisted on driving himself,' she recalls frankly.

Bobby was blind drunk behind the wheel and, as he tried to navigate his way home, he got lost. Shirley decided she wanted to get out of the car because she knew that if she got out, she could ring Stan Mellor because he was nearby and she knew he would take her down to Lambourn.

But then, in an incident that shocked even Bobby (albeit much later, after he had sobered up), she stumbled when she got out of the car and Bobby nearly reversed over her. He even left a tyre mark on her coat.

'He was fighting with me on the side of the road and trying to get me back into the car and I said I wouldn't unless I was driving. I drew out and hit him that time. Although it says in his book that I had a wicked left hook, I didn't – I had a wicked right hook. And I drew blood. When he saw the blood he was as quiet as could be, so I took the car keys from him and I drove home. I told him the next day that if he ever laid a finger on me again then I was gone.'

This was not the only bizarre incident between the two:

one day Shirley was pottering away at home when Bobby had a completely inexplicable moment. 'Our house in Lambourn had a long kitchen at the back of it,' she remembers vividly. 'There was a wooden window by the kitchen sink and there was a conservatory around the back door. I was watering the plants one day and he was up in the kitchen making a sandwich or something, and he threw this knife and it stuck in the window right beside me. I said to myself, "If he doesn't kill me, I will kill him. And if he does kill me, he'll get away with it because he's drunk but if I kill him, I won't because I'm sober."'

Bobby returned to racing on the following 31 January and his mount fell. Fred Winter was doing his best to pick and choose suitable rides for his ostensible number one jockey, but coming towards the end of the season there was an incident at Windsor where Bobby had the mounts on three well-fancied runners and lost on all of them. He'd had a few drinks beforehand and admitted to being 'terrible' on the day. His reflexes had gone and his strength too. Once again Shirley was taking flak for all of this – although it was patently not her fault – and soon too she would be gone.

She remembers Bobby storming out of the house one night ranting that she would not talk to him. That night he met another woman and soon after he was the talk of Lambourn.

'I knew he had a girlfriend – who he called Joyce in his book, but that was not her name,' Shirley says. 'That was the first time we split up in Lambourn and he was supposed to be marrying her and everything. He'd had a few others before that too, but I knew it would not last very long.'

Bobby maintains that in 'Joyce' he had found someone who was prepared to shower him with the affection and love he craved. Two rebukes from Fred Winter were not enough to stop the madness. The trainer initially told him he did not want him mixing in the village and drinking there. Bobby ignored him. Later, and after a furious row between Shirley and himself over his new girlfriend, Fred intervened once more and told Bobby he was an alcoholic and needed help. Amazingly, he also told him that if he did get help, his job would be there for him the following season.

Once more Bobby ignored him and to his dying day he maintained it was his 'greatest regret' that he did not take the advice of a man 'so tolerant, kind, good and loyal'.

Shortly after that, he arrived home roaring drunk one afternoon and told Shirley to 'get out of my f★★★★★g life'. She accepted the offer.

'I was packing my little Ford Anglia car and he was throwing clothes at me and everything like that and I just drove away. As I was driving away he threw a tenner into the car to me in case I needed money. So I went to Stan and Elaine and then William and Susan [Robinson] rang up telling me Bobby was going around Lambourn saying he was going to make the kids wards of court, so it might be better if I could get them out of the country. As it happened, the Robinsons were travelling to Ireland with the car and I had to meet them in Stow-in-the-Wold at six in the morning, dump the kids in and tell my mother and father to meet the boat at the far end, which they did.

'I stayed in England with Stan and Elaine, and Stan insisted I go to a solicitor, which I did, and then I came back home to be reunited with the children. As an only child, there was no problem with my coming back to my parents place in Camolin,' she said.

Bobby was disconsolate and because he was blaming anyone but himself for his woes, he was not helping himself in any way. Although he was still riding the odd horse here and there, he was left licking his wounds and his drinking intensified alarmingly. To his credit, Fred Winter contacted Bobby and asked him to ride out in the mornings, but this was only a temporary fillip as Richard Pitman remembers it as a time when Bobby pretty much disintegrated.

'When he did fall apart it was terrible. He was on his own and he was in that rented cottage up the Maddle Road in Upper Lambourn, which is in the middle of nowhere. In fact, there is nothing at the end of the road where he was – just thousands of acres of farmland. Bobby would come out and ride two lots in the morning and then disappear back to the cottage with a bottle of vodka and go to bed if he was not racing. It was very sad to see. Certainly people knew what was happening because they could see it in front of their eyes.'

Back in Ireland, Shirley and the children were still with her parents. There was no initial contact with Bobby, but there was plenty of news filtering through to her from Lambourn – not all of it good.

'After about a month or so, Bobby was on to me telling me how sorry he was and all that sort of thing. He told me he was giving up the drink and all that. Of course, what happened was that we got back together again. He did crazy things then, but he didn't give up the drink and he was flitting back and forward to England. He bought a little place just up the road here in Wexford with a few acres of land. We had some people living in the house for a while, renting it.'

However obvious it may have been to others that their relationship was ultimately doomed, Shirley went back to England to try to make the marriage work. It failed and Shirley herself reckons she was foolish to have believed otherwise. She had, after all, seen the extremes to which Bobby could go and had lived through some genuinely terrifying moments.

'There were times when Bobby used to shout and scream at me that he'd break my spirit, but all I'd think to myself was "you bloody well won't". I think it was the Yorkshire blood in me,' she recalls. 'It was a bit of a crazy time and I think I went a bit peculiar myself at times. I was lucky that I did have some good friends.'

Not really aware of what he was doing, Bobby was back and forth between Ireland and Lambourn. Unbelievably, Fred Winter was still entertaining him at this point and Bobby rode a winner for him on a horse called Rimmon at Fontwell on 7 May. It was, he later said, 'the most horrible ride I've ever had'. It took him some two hours to recover from his exertions; he had half collapsed after dismounting the horse and then his hands locked as he tried to undo his girth straps. He decided to retire on the spot and went to Uplands the following morning to tell Fred Winter. Fred, kindness personified, offered him the ride on a certainty in a chase, saying it would be a nice way for Bobby 'to go out', but he would not accept the ride. Instead he chose another horse for his final ride and it ran a bad third.

According to Terry Biddlecombe, it was not a shock when Bobby retired. 'He only had one yard to ride for and he did not get many outside rides apart from one or two coming from Ireland. We would have known the depths of his problem. Fred mightn't have had a clue, but the rest of the boys knew well what was going on. I used to go to parties with him and it was very strange because initially it seemed he had no manners. He used to give a lot of abuse to people – myself included – but I accepted that back then because I was only a kid and I used to laugh at him,' he says.

While Bobby was waiting for the furniture removers to come and empty the Maddle Road house, Fred Winter also asked him to ride out each morning just to pass the time. He did and grew a particular affinity for one recently-broken young horse in particular and told the trainer he thought this particular beast was the real deal. Whatever else Bobby had lost at this point, it was not his ability to judge good animals. The horse in question turned out to be a future Champion Hurdle winner and subsequent star chaser. His name was Bula, and Bobby, unbeknownst to himself or anyone else at this point, would be seeing a lot more of him.

★

The day after Bobby's retirement was announced in the newspapers, he received a letter from a London-based insurance firm asking him if he would like to sell policies for them. Obviously looking to tap into his sporting contacts, they were unaware what they were actually tapping into. He was offered £20 a week for his endeavours and was told that he would start work a month later.

In the meantime he headed back to Ireland and – despite everything that had gone before – he and Shirley were reconciled. Bobby was still drinking heavily, but the couple sensed 'a glimmer of a chance' that the marriage might be saved. Bobby maintained that, freed from the pressures of Lambourn – and particularly from the 'piss pills' – he became 'loving and persuasive' and Shirley conceived again with their third child, Helen.

However, the managers in the insurance company were beginning to wonder where their new ace salesman was and, after several false starts caused by a crisis of confidence and fear of loneliness, Bobby duly returned to England to try and forge a new start. It was a disaster.

Cold-calling was a non-starter for him, but he managed to

sell a few policies to his former weighroom colleagues. Richard Pitman was one.

'I bought an insurance policy off Bobby,' he says. 'That was a very sad, sad thing. There he was, my hero, riding out for Fred Winter and the next day he's coming around selling insurance. Now I am a very wet character, so of course I bought a policy off him. I didn't want him to have to go through the whole spiel he had been given, so I took it off him straight away. I cashed it in when I got divorced, in case it became a bone of contention afterwards. But what a difficult transition that must have been – that sort of thing was certainly not in his nature or in his blood. It must have been terrible for him.'

Bobby's new job selling insurance did not last long and he returned to Wexford, where he noted that while a paralytic drunk was an object of disgust in England, back at home he was regarded simply as a hard man and a hard drinker.

Amongst his best drinking friends at this point was Nicky Rackard, a member of the legendary Wexford hurling family and a veterinarian. Rackard, however, was also a hard man and a hard drinker and the two got into several scrapes.

Shirley remembers one night when the two of them arrived back to her house and caused havoc.

'We just started getting into this same pattern again. I remember one night I heard this helluva racket downstairs and the two of them were there eating raw sausages and mushrooms – everything straight out of the fridge. I went down and told them to get the hell out of there. Nicky actually made a swing at me but he put his fist through the door. Later on Nicky wanted to replace the door, but I told him I would not let him and I would tell anyone who asked how the door got damaged. It was still that way when I left the house.'

One night – as far as Nicky Rackard was concerned, anyway

– it all came to a head. After three days' solid drinking he told Bobby that he was thinking of ending it all and taking his own life. Bobby was horrified and angry. He told his friend that, while he had lost everything and had nothing to look forward to, Rackard was, on the other hand, a professional man who could always go back to his veterinary work when he was cured. The very next day Nicky Rackard admitted himself to hospital.

Proud of his work with his friend, Bobby obstinately refused to admit that he too had a problem. He knew he had one, but simply would not admit it.

There were, however, other forces at work and he was beginning to feel their influence.

Christy – Baby Days

Captain Christy was born in the spring of 1967 at the modest Carrignaveen Stud just outside Inniscarra in the beautiful Lee Valley area just a few miles west of Cork city. His breeder was George Williams who maintains that, in terms of the breeding of horses, he had taken inspiration from a certain Captain Horace Holroyd Smith, the owner – before his death in 1969 – of the huge Ballynatray Estate outside Youghal in the east of the county.

Williams, a small time breeder, dealer and trainer, held Holroyd Smith in high esteem and, as a willing listener and learner, he was only too willing to take advice on bloodlines from anyone more expert than himself.

'He used to have his accounts kept by Jack Williams, a relative of mine and that's how I connected up with him,' Williams recalls. 'I heard him talking to Corney Barry – another authority on horses – and they maintained that if you could cross the blood of White Knight with My Prince that it would be the best cross you could get as almost every Grand National winner had that sort of a cross in them.'

It might seem mundane to anyone outside the breeding loop, but George Williams was on the trail of the Holy Grail

– that vision of a successful racing beast – as were most of his contemporaries.

'Now, I already had Mon Capitaine and his dam was by My Prince so I set out to find the blood of the White Knight. He was, of course, dead by then and the next horse I could find from the same bloodline was Bowsprit. I went up to the sales and, buying within my small limit, I got a little mare – she was a butty little thing – for about £300 or £400. I brought her home and broke her with the intention of trying to get her to win a race. I called her Christy's Bow and she was a three-year-old when I got her. But she turned out to be as slow as a wet week and when we galloped her my late wife could pass her on a half-bred hunter, so there was no real point in following that line of endeavour. She was a dead loss as a racehorse.

'Anyway, the next time she came in season she was covered by Mon Capitaine and her first foal was Captain Christy. But the turn of events was fortunate at best. I had got Mon Capitaine when I was breaking a half-bred horse for a local farmer here in Inniscarra and I was riding him just up the road from the house here when along came a brown Volkswagen and who was in it only Ted and Ruby Walsh.'

Ruby Walsh, father of Ted and grandfather of his namesake and top jockey Ruby, and his brother Ted were from Fermoy in County Cork. They trained there and also maintained a long-standing family tradition of buying and selling horses.

'They were there admiring the horse I was on, but I told them I'd like something a bit faster and they responded, saying, "Maybe we've something that might suit you." They had taken Mon Capitaine as a kind of a part-exchange with another horse and they wanted to move him on and that's how I got him. He was never really going to be a racer at that stage, as far as I was concerned, but he was an entire horse and I put him to stud straight away.'

Indeed, Mon Capitaine had been a racehorse in France and Ireland and had been bred in France by the sire of many famous French jumpers, Wild Risk. He was a moderate racecourse performer at best but did win in France over a mile before being sent to Ireland as a four-year-old to be trained by Paddy Prendergast. He finished last in two flat races before being sent hurdling where, over the course of six seasons, he scored two modest wins.

Ted Walsh relates the circumstances as to how Mon Capitaine came to be passed on by his father and uncle to George Williams.

'Mon Capitaine was owned by a woman called Barbara Harcourt-Wood who lived in a place called Glengiblin, outside Fermoy, and local man Bill Roche was sort of training for her because back in that time women could not have a licence in their own name. She had plenty of money and Bill was down to be the trainer and he trained Mon Capitaine. But then in the early '60s she decided to pack up and go back to England. The two lads – Ruby and Ted – ended up with Mon Capitaine and I remember him being in the yard – a big, noisy, liver-chestnut horse who used to roar his head off if anyone came into the place, not unlike a son he would eventually have. He was a well-bred horse – a French bred – and George Williams was very friendly with my father and my uncle, simply, I suppose, because they were horsemen living in roughly the same neck of the woods in Cork.

'George was looking for a stallion and he ended up buying Mon Capitaine off the lads. There would have been wheeling and dealing (that was all part of the scene back then) because the two boys were into buying and selling horses – point-to-pointers, show horses, all sorts of horses. Their father had started buying troopers for the army back in the First World War, but the horsey business is a small business anyway and everyone knew everyone else.

'Mon Capitaine was by a horse called Wild Risk, a very good French horse and one that was popular ever before French pedigrees came more to the fore. Frank Latham had a few stallions – Vulgan and Fortria – and they were French-bred. The French lines are very popular now, but even at that time French pedigrees were popular for breeding jumpers. They were valued. Mon Capitaine was an all-right racehorse without being a star, but he was left intact and in his latter days he got very "stalliony" and he didn't do a lot of racing towards the end of his career.'

As a stallion, however, Mon Capitaine was about to make his mark by producing one of the greatest national hunt horses ever seen.

George Williams sold Mon Capitaine's foal at Tattersalls' Ballsbridge sales for 290 guineas to Tom Nicholson and says without equivocation that he was 'not unhappy leaving Dublin that day'. He sold three other foals as well the same day and reckons 'the 290 guineas I got for Christy was very nearly the top lot for a colt foal, if I remember. So I was quite pleased with the business I did.'

The Nicholsons too were happy with the deal. John, Tom's son, says that on the day his father bought the horse, he was accompanied by the legendary Paddy Mullins, who would later train Dawn Run to her unique Champion Hurdle/Gold Cup double. Tom has carried on the family tradition of breeding and training horses at their home farm at Knockdav, just outside Johnstown in County Kilkenny.

'My father and Paddy were very close and Paddy trained Vulpine for us to win the Irish Grand National in 1967. The two of them were wonderful judges of an animal and when this

Mon Capitaine colt was brought into the ring, they were both immediately impressed. My father knew nothing about Mon Capitaine, but he said to Paddy, "I really like the walk of that horse and the look of him, but I know nothing about the sire."

'Paddy Mullins said to him, "If I had your land, I'd buy him too. He's a grand stamp of a horse." My father hadn't even seen him walk around outside, but he just liked what he had seen and he bought him for 290 guineas. He later went down to the stables to look at the horse again. It was in the evening and there was no electricity in the stables, but my father, who was not a smoking man, had a box of matches and he lit one up for a bit of light and didn't the horse nearly jump out through the roof!'

Tony O'Hehir reckons that Christy's purchase by the Nicholsons could only have been a good thing for the horse, given their record in the racing game.

'The Nicholsons had some very good horses down the years. They had Bigaroon, which won the Cesarewitch three times and they also had Chinrullah, who they sold on to Mick O'Toole. They always had good horses and Tom Nicholson also owned Vulpine who won the Irish Grand National when trained by Paddy Mullins. So it was no bad thing that the foal went to them,' he says.

This view is endorsed by Tos Taaffe. 'The Nicholsons were very respected and they were hardy people,' he maintains. 'They always had good horses and they knew what to do with them.'

The horse was taken back to Kilkenny where the Nicholsons 'threw the horse away for a few years' and 'fed the lard out of him'. Nicholson senior liked the horse so much that he made contact with George Williams and sent several mares to be covered by Mon Capitaine, even before the still unnamed Captain Christy had ever seen a racecourse. 'We liked our fella a lot and as we got to know about the breeding of Mon

Capitaine, we decided to get more involved with him as a sire,' John Nicholson recounts.

However much the Nicholsons liked the horse and the potential he showed, they knew he was a fractious sort and would pose difficulties as he matured.

'We brought in the horse to break him as a three-year-old and, by Jesus, he was a terrible horse to break. He was the toughest horse that was ever broken here. Even now when we have a tough horse and are breaking him, I still say there was nothing as bad as Captain Christy. He nearly killed what men were in the place – he was unbelievable. It was said in Ivor Herbert's *Winter Kings* that "legs were broken" when we tried to break Christy and while I wouldn't say it went as far as that, it was damn near it.

'Tom Bergin – Tom who used to train down this way – used to work with us and he broke the horse, which had to be starved to break him, he was that headstrong. When we did eventually get him riding, he was still unpredictable. I remember we were out doing a bit of road work one day and the horse jumped up on a ditch and threw Tom Bergin to the ground. Then he damn near walked on top of him and nearly killed him.

'We did master him eventually, but there was no denying he was a tough horse. He was a lovely block of a horse and had a lovely sharp head on him. He was also a lovely mover and he showed an awful lot of promise here as a three-year-old, even if he was unpredictable. We got him going in the spring of that year and when we brought him on, we felt we had something good all right.'

This was a judgement that the Nicholsons were not alone in making. Four people who would later play roles in the horse's future – Tos Taaffe, Ted Walsh, Jimmy Kelly and Pat Murphy – also saw a lot to like in Christy's physique.

Tos Taaffe recalls a beast who, while headstrong, was a good looking animal, if not exceptional. 'He was a fair looker,' he says, 'and he was a bay horse, but even so there was nothing about him that stood him out. His breeding was nothing exceptional, but he certainly put George Williams on the map. He was a hardy individual, but to look at him there was no greatness about him, I'd say.'

For his part Ted Walsh remembers Christy as being some 16.3 hands high but straight of his shoulder and a bit short of his front.

'He was not a typical top chaser. I mean Kauto Star has a long front and Denman has a long front; Desert Orchid too had a long front. The Captain had a high head carriage and that meant that even though he had a shortish front, he made it shorter by the fact he didn't stretch his head out. He was a good stamp of a horse and there was plenty of power about him. There was a great rear end on him and that made him a very strong horse. He was big, but short coupled. He was not a gangly horse, because there was plenty of him. In Irish rugby terms he was more of a Keith Wood than a Paul O'Connell. He was an athlete – a great mover – but he was stocky,' he says.

Jimmy Kelly, Pat Taaffe's veterinarian and a former champion sportsman in his own right, having been capped eleven times for Ireland in rugby in the 1960s, remembers him well.

'He was a big horse and a tough horse to do anything with,' he says. 'If you were giving him electrolytes or anything – trying to earn your few bob – he was tough. But having said that, I remember Elaine, Pat's youngest daughter, at four or five years of age and she could be up on Christy's back while he was walking around the yard. He was himself and he was a hell of a horse. He was one of those horses we all hope we breed – one of the ones that keeps us breeding. You think you are going to beat the odds, but by and large you don't. I remember one time bringing the late Professor O'Connor from the Vet College down to old Joe Osborne, Robbie's grandfather, for him to give a second opinion on something. Afterwards Joe brought us in for a cup of tea and O'Connor was asking him what was the first thing he looked for in a horse. Joe responded with one word "Pedigree". Christy didn't really have much pedigree but that's how it goes sometimes.'

Pat Murphy, later a successful trainer in his own right in the UK, would meet Christy when the horse eventually came under Pat Taaffe's charge and he reckons that while Christy was a tall horse, he was not the most robust horse in the world.

'He was nothing like, say, the Dreaper horses of old, which Pat Taaffe would have been used to riding in his racing career. These would have been big strapping animals, bred for a different era of racing; Christy was much more athletic looking than them. In fact, for a lot of his life you could have looked at him and said he had a lot more maturing to do. There was always a lot of daylight underneath him and he never carried a whole heap of condition, but was always well-muscled. He did, for a lot of the time, have quite a high head carriage and we used to put it down to the fact that he didn't want to miss anything that might be going on over the hedges. But, if you compare him to some of the good Irish horses of the time – the likes of Ten Up and Brown Lad and those (they were big old-fashioned chasers) – Christy could never, ever, be described as an old-fashioned chaser.

'I have a great vision of Christy with The Dikler on the run-in at Cheltenham and do you know The Dikler was different in every way? He dwarfed him in every way; he was taller, he was longer, broader and Christy looked like a flaming pony beside him, to be honest.

'Christy was very athletic and much more the modern-day chaser than what we had back then in general, which were big, strong, deep-girthed horses. You could never describe Christy as any of those things. But trainers would love him today because he was so athletic. Maybe he was the first of a generation.'

Whatever about those opinions of the horse, John Nicholson is very proud of the fact that that it was on the one-and-a-half-mile uphill gallop on his family's farm that Christy got his initial training. John feels that the stamina he gained as a result of the work he did on that hill stood to him throughout his career.

'Over the years we won an awful lot of four-year-old bumpers because the horses were always really fit because they were trained naturally up that hill. We had that gallop before anyone had any all-weather gallops and we still train them the same way and are still able to get our few winners. We never put in an all-weather and that gallop is the very same one that we trained Christy on. You can go right out to the top of the hill, which is the highest point in County Kilkenny at 1,850 feet above sea level,' he says.

But before they could start training him, the horse had to be named. In choosing a name the Nicholsons did not stray too far from common practice by combining elements of the names of the sire and the dam and so it was that the progeny of Mon Capitaine and Christy's Bow became officially registered with the Irish Turf Club as Captain Christy.

Comeback

Bobby Beasley was still drinking heavily when he made his return to race riding. Although he had managed to persuade his friend and drinking partner Nicky Rackard that he badly needed help (advice which Rackard eventually took), Bobby himself continued on as normal – or at least what was normal for him.

With Shirley having had their third child, Helen, and the couple enjoying a somewhat renewed relationship, things seemed to be going all right, but the truth was that Bobby was deluding himself into believing he could carry on as he wished.

Bobby was still very much in denial about the depth of his own problems, but felt that forces were at work that would ultimately prove to be his salvation.

First there came an offer from Dublin auctioneer and permit holder Stuart Barrett for Bobby to come to his base in Portmarnock to help him train the seven racehorses he owned. Bobby agreed but on the basis that he would not ride any of the horses. He had, he maintained, a mental block and would not get on a horse's back.

After about a month at Barrett's, Bobby had something of a Damascene moment one day on the way to the races in Navan when 'something stirred' in him and he suddenly blurted out, 'I'll start riding on Monday.' True to his word, he did just that and immediately reported it seemed like he'd stopped riding only the day before.

A number of other jockeys were called in to ride work and cast an eye over Bobby and while one reckoned he was badly overweight, but otherwise seemed OK in the saddle, the other got Bobby's dander up by telling him not to bother making a comeback because he was too old.

He decided there was no time like the present and applied to the registry office in Dublin for a jockey's licence. Although still downing a steady quota of booze – 'because I had to have it' – he believed there were no moral grounds to deny him his licence, even if there were genuine medical concerns.

That being the case, the stewards insisted that he receive a medical check-up and this was where he first encountered the respected endocrinologist Dr Austin Darragh.

His introduction to the good doctor was the start of a life-changing experience for Bobby and, as Darragh himself recalls, it was Stuart Barrett who got the ball rolling.

He remembers Barrett wanting to discuss Bobby's case with him as he felt there was a lot the doctor could do for him. Darragh had already been involved in helping to cure weight issues for a number of UK-based riders, not least of which was the well-known flat jockey Duncan Keith.

Darragh's expertise in this area had arisen through a curious set of circumstances, not all of which would sit comfortably with Bobby's renewed hatred of the Roman Catholic Church. Bobby was so knotted up about the Church that if he thought his treatment had resulted from research that allowed women to comply with *Humanae Vitae* while not getting pregnant, he would have been distinctly unimpressed. 'I had taken an appointment with Mother Mary Martin in the Lourdes Hospital in Drogheda,' Darragh says, 'and one of the things which was bothering us at the time was that oral contraception was being condemned by *Humanae Vitae* [an encyclical letter on birth control from Pope Paul VI in 1968] and it seemed logical that there was some other way of controlling fertility more reliably than just with the safe period, the thermometer and the rosary beads,' he recalls.

'I believed that it would be possible – as a result of other research work I was doing with the pharmaceutical industry – to regulate ovulation. Instead of suppressing ovulation the idea was to make it happen and then two days later the woman was safe. To do this I needed to get access to women who had an intact mechanism – a pituitary/ovarian mechanism – which had been switched off for some reason. The one condition where this happens as a feature is anorexia nervosa where suffering women lose their periods. They have all the equipment, but it is switched off higher up by influences which are not working on the pituitary.

'So we had an obstetrical unit in the Lourdes hospital, but they only saw about two or three cases of anorexia nervosa a year. In the meantime, Mother Mary brought me to meet Cardinal Conway in Armagh and explained to him my idea about how women could conform to *Humanae Vitae* and he gave us his blessing in our endeavours.

'Later on I was at a party one night and I met [prominent psychiatrist] Ivor Browne and he asked me what I was up to and I explained that I was looking for anorexia nervosa cases. He said had a ward full of thirty-six of them in St Brendan's Hospital. I was then appointed as a consultant endocrinologist to the Eastern Health Board and we made a lot of progress and within eighteen months I had that ward cleared out. So I had acquired a certain skill in dealing with anorexia nervosa, as well as nutrition and metabolism.

'I then got permission to take blood from nuns and nurses through their whole cycle to see what was happening. To know that a woman had ovulated I would want to know that progesterone was going up in the bloodstream, so I had to develop a test for progesterone. I was working away at this and I also developed a method whereby horse owners could blood-test mares to see if they were in foal – thus saving time and money on stallions,' Darragh says.

The corollary was that in making these discoveries about how to get people back to full health from a condition such as anorexia nervosa, he also – and more importantly for many jockeys, not least of whom would be Bobby – discovered how to manage weight issues.

'News of this somehow reached England and I got a call from a trainer in England who said he had a very talented jockey called Duncan Keith who was suffering from weight problems. I got him sent over and, as it turned out, it was a doddle because he was hyperthyroid. I took him into a little hospital in Cabinteely to keep an eye on him and I also got him a job riding work at Seamus McGrath's yard which was nearby.

'I started treating him carefully for the thyroid and he got fit again. We got him down to about eight stone from twelve-and-a-half and he went back and immediately scored a string of good results. He was interviewed in the *Sunday Times* and he said that he had been over to Ireland to a strange little doctor over there. After that jockeys started to come over from England big time.

'People then knew I could do something about obesity and that was how Stuart Barrett approached me to see if I could help Bobby and I said I would. I have to say that he was not in

great condition when I first saw him – he was very fat, about
fifteen stone, I'd say. He was also very flat in himself and he
didn't think there was any future for his career. I knew from
my experience with jockeys the punishment they were putting
themselves through to maintain weights that were more relevant
to the sixteenth and seventeenth centuries – taking things like
Lasix and diuretics and becoming short on potassium.

'Bobby was depressed because his career – which, to me, he
loved – was in tatters, the alcohol was also a factor and there
were also marital problems. But my part in it was only doing
the job I was supposed to do – to retrieve him as a human
being. People have to be helped back. He was so depleted of
electrolytes, vitamins and morale; he needed a lot of things.
He also needed prayer and I don't think he was completely
removed from prayer. While he did not necessarily embrace the
fact he was going to be in a convent, there was an atmosphere
there where the inexplicable effect of prayer can help people,'
Darragh maintains.

Bobby himself recalled that the clinic was staffed by excellent
nursing nuns from a French Order 'who put me to bed and
took blood tests, cardiographs and all sorts of other things'.

'Having renounced the Pope and all his works,' he said later,
'I felt a bit uptight about the nuns. They were good to me,
however, and did what they could to ease my depression. My
mind was willing – even wanting – to have a go, but I was
feeling terribly low physically. I had no energy at all.

'As a result of his tests, Darragh discovered that all of the
Saluric, Hydro-saluric and Lasix tablets, as well as the alcohol,
had completely dehydrated me, turned my metabolism upside
down and taken away all the electrolytes, so that my nervous
system was shot to pieces. He said there was nothing left. He
also realised – and I took it from him, albeit reluctantly – that

I was an alcoholic, but he did not recommend Alcoholics Anonymous.'

Bobby threw himself fully into Darragh's expert hands and accepted the ministrations of both the doctor and the nuns. And, in Darragh's considered view, the religious nature of the hospital did Bobby good spiritually, even if the jockey did not think so.

'It does not matter whether you're talking to a Jew, a Hindu, a Buddhist, a Mohammedan,' Darragh says. 'The good force which can be transferred from one person to another through the power of wishing well is extraordinary.'

The bottom line, he maintains, is that whether or not Bobby liked being in a convent, 'The positivity in the environment certainly did him good. A person like him, who was of the opinion that he did not need God, was still a nett benefactor of the prayer and the goodwill around him,' Darragh felt.

'I don't know how many times I have seen things in my career in medicine, which happen only because they're due to other influences which we are too ignorant to know about. I have seen the power of prayer in so many different ways – both in my own personal life and in my dealings with patients of various creeds,' he maintains.

'Bobby was imbued with an internal desire to get back to where he had been and he was committed to utilising his God-given gift. One of the main reasons he had gone so far downhill was because he was criticising himself internally for not achieving what he was meant to achieve.

'There were a lot of interconnected things going on – and the mess of his personal life was one of them. It would be impossible for anyone to blame Shirley for the way his life was; you would have to see that he was not making it easy for anyone to love him in any way. He was ultimately very lucky that someone like Pat Taaffe recognised the one big attribute he had – which was as a brilliant horseman – and he could see there was something worthwhile in Bobby.

'I would contrast him with Barry Brogan, who was also an absolutely brilliant horseman, but did not have the same inner strength which was so clearly imbued in Bobby. I got the feeling from Stuart Barrett from the outset that he had tremendous belief in Bobby. I actually got the feeling later that Barrett had Captain Christy in mind for Bobby even when he came and talked to me. That is what I feel. I think he thought that this was a man who could come back and be a champion and it was worth making the effort to get him right. Barrett certainly had enormous belief in him, which probably was reinforced by Pat Taaffe. But the bottom line is that Bobby's story is a story of human courage.'

Richard Pitman and Bobby met in the Cheltenham Gold Cup in 1974 but before then, Richard was another of Austin Darragh's patients. He recalls the experience of being treated by the Irish doctor as a relatively painless one.

'Whoever put me on to Austin Darragh – and it probably was Bobby, because the timescale is right – I certainly needed to see him. I was quite a blocky, chunky lad and I suppose as I became more successful, I eased off the gas a little bit in terms of what I used to do to keep the weight down,' he recalls.

'In my early days I would ride out in the morning and then go for a run to raise a sweat. Then, if I was racing, I would put on a sweat suit and put on a tracksuit over it, get into the car and drive all the way to the races with the heater on. It was mad and it was bloody dangerous as well. You'd get out of the car in Newton Abbot or somewhere and there would be water pouring out the legs of the tracksuit. How the hell can that be right?

'Anyway, I went to see Darragh and I went there thinking that he'd find something – "it's your thyroid gland" – give me an injection and I'd be two stone lighter. I remember the place being called the "psycho-endocrine clinic". What they would do was, they would put you to sleep at five in the evening after giving you a glucose drink. Then you would be woken up twelve hours later by the prettiest nurse who would take a urine sample. 'After that you'd go back to sleep and they'd monitor you then every half hour or hour to keep an eye on the sugar levels in the body. About the fourth time they woke you, it wasn't a pretty nurse any more, it was a tough one. Giving blood was easy, but peeing was very difficult, especially after the fourth one. They spent two days testing everything: brain, lungs, thyroid, liver – the whole lot. They tested everything that could possibly have anything to do with weight gain and at the end of the two days you'd be brought into Austin Darragh's personal office, which was very plush, and he'd sit you down and say, "I am afraid to tell you …" And you're there going "oh my God, it's my heart. I knew something was wrong …" And he'd say, "No, no dear fellow, you've just got very lazy and I want you to exercise more".'

'After that you signed the cheque and were sent on your way with a set of instructions as to what he wanted you to do. In my case, he wanted me to walk for an hour in the mornings. He ruled out running as I have bulky thighs and running would only build them up. But it was a lovely eye-opening experience. If you could ride even just 2 lb less than your minimum, it increases the number of rides you get by a substantial margin.'

Bobby was not concerned about increasing the number of rides he could get. He just wanted to be able to ride again. Full stop. Neither did he consider his efforts to be a 'story of human courage' as Austin Darragh did. His jaundiced view of himself and the world he lived in prevented any real sense of well-being. And, incredibly, he did not even consider giving up the drink.

The treatment he was receiving consisted of injections of Parentrovite, a complex multivitamin, as well as Vitamin B12, which were aimed at replacing his lost electrolytes. Buoyed by the treatment, he also signed up with Eddie Downey, an ex-boxer who had a health clinic in the Montrose Hotel. His weight was down to 10 stone 5 lb and he was convinced that he had proved to himself and others that he had 'knocked off the booze, or at least, that I can control it'. That, unfortunately, would take a little more time. With Darragh's blessing, the turf authorities granted Bobby a licence to ride under Irish National Hunt Rules on 21 December 1970, and the following day *The Irish Times* reported that 'one of National Hunt Racing's most stylish jockeys' would make his return to the track at Limerick the following 28 December. That day he rode a horse owned and trained by Stuart Barrett called Gordon and although the horse and jockey were unplaced, at least Bobby was back in business. Initially wary of the reception he might get at tracks around the country, he gradually got back into the rhythm of race-riding and the daily routine that is a jockey's life.

Pat Murphy, who subsequently became a successful trainer in his own right, was working in Taaffe's yard at the time and has his own take on Bobby's return.

'You can make jockeys, but you can't make horsemen,' he says. 'So when Bobby returned you had a man who had a God-given talent as a horseman. You can finesse a jockey and he can learn with experience and all that sort of thing, but the actual horsemanship is something you're born with. When he did come back, Bobby did not look any different in the saddle than he had before being forced to retire. In fact, the level of fitness he got himself back to was incredible. He was way ahead of his time in that respect. Nowadays guys have gyms, they have nutritionists, fitness instructors and so forth. Once he got the help he needed from Austin Darragh, it was largely down to himself at that point. Darragh was the closest thing to a nutritionist/fitness adviser that Bobby had back then and he was way ahead of his time. But even with that support, it was going to take fantastic willpower on Bobby's behalf to get him back to racing fitness. The others that Darragh had helped were all still riding at the time. Bobby was not. Here was a guy who had been to the brink – perhaps over it even – but he still had enough about him and he was enough of a man to be able to see, firstly, what he wanted to do and, secondly, how to go about achieving it. That was the great thing about Bobby and that is why he deserved the successes he had with Captain Christy and others when he did return.

'Going back to the late '60s and early '70s people in their thirties now would have no appreciation of the difference in life then to how it is now. There were not the facilities to do anything other than bloody hard graft. Neither the technology nor the knowledge that exists now, existed then. Healthy food, for example, as we now know it, was not even invented back then. It was always assumed that various things were bad for your weight, but they turned out to be essential ingredients in a healthy diet.

'What was amazing about Bobby was how quickly he was able to get himself back into it. Even nowadays, you'll get a jockey who has had a lengthy injury lay off and they will tell you themselves it takes ages to get back your feel for the timing or the pace of a race. Bobby just seemed to step back into it like he had never left. There didn't seem to be any transitional period for him – he was bang on the button from day one. He was an incredible jockey as well as a horseman. Yes, the horseman was still able to get the horses jumping, travelling and generally thinking the job out. But the jockey bit was also needed to judge the tempo of a race – "Are we going a strong gallop?" "Are we going an ordinary gallop?" "When is it time to kick?" All that sort of stuff. That generally is something you only get from race-riding, but with Bobby, incredibly, it was right there when he did come back. Maybe he just managed to blot out all the time he had missed.'

Bobby's return was not made any easier when one English paper printed a front-page story about his comeback – written by an Irish journalist – which essentially advised him to stay retired and also, by implication, advised owners and trainers not to engage him. It was a story which would remain very definitely not only in Bobby's own mind, but also in that of his fellow professionals and the Irish racing media.

In any event, Bobby finished third – again aboard Gordon – at Thurles on Wednesday 6 January and there followed further unsuccessful rides at Leopardstown, Gowran and Tramore, as the jockey tried to find his feet again in a world which he had deserted.

Then he got a phone call from his rehabilitating friend Nicky Rackard telling him that jockey Francis Shortt was injured and his old friend Paddy Murphy – who had given him his first Grand National ride on Sandy Jane – needed a replacement.

Shirley Beasley remembers the occasion well. 'When we tried to get back together and we did up the house and moved in, I remember Nicky coming over one night to say that poor Francis Shortt had broken his leg and Paddy Murphy wanted Bobby to ride Norwegian Flag.'

Bobby himself would report later that it was at this very moment he knew the time had come to kick the drink.

'Darragh was helping me; Eddie Downey was helping me; Stuart Barrett was helping me; and now Paddy Murphy was going to give me a chance. This was my moment of truth. I knew for the first time that I didn't just drink too much – I was actually powerless to control it by myself and must seek help to knock it on the head and stop it for once and for all.'

He attended four different meetings of Alcoholics Anonymous with Nicky Rackard before he felt able to commit. He felt self-righteous and he felt that all those others who stood up at the meetings and admitted their failing were somehow different from him and he singularly failed to identify with them.

At the fifth meeting, however, he finally got it; he finally admitted to himself he needed help. 'My name is Bobby,' he told the meeting. 'I am an alcoholic.' He had overcome the 'biggest barrier of all' and confessed to having the disease.

The floodgates opened and Bobby told the meeting 'as far as I could remember, all I had done was wreck my life'. It was most certainly an emotional time for him and he later admitted that the biggest problem he had to master 'was the guilt and the remorse for the frightful emotional damage I had done to my wife and our marriage'. That guilt would live with him for a very long time.

Even so, Shirley was simply relieved that he had decided to accept help and she has no doubt who was largely responsible for this welcome sea change in him. 'When he put himself in with Austin Darragh and started to try and get himself back together, that was definitely the moment for me. I believe Darragh definitely did get him off the booze, no doubt about it.'

However, she does credit Paddy Murphy and Nicky Rackard for their role, saying, 'We were very friendly with Paddy Murphy and he and his wife Gwen were down here with us a lot. But the thing was that Paddy knew Bobby still had the knack of riding well – he still had it. If only he could have kept his head right. And when Bobby eventually did the AA thing and Nicky got him to go, you felt that there was real momentum behind him to kick the drink.'

Even so, she says she did not see any immediate change. Certainly, there was the bonus that her husband no longer got violent and was not as pushy as he had been either, but his moods were difficult to cope with. 'Nicky used to say to me "he's stopped drinking, but he has not changed his attitude to people",' she says.

In terms of his return to racing, it was not until Saturday 20 February that Bobby broke his duck and, appropriately, it came at Leopardstown, the scene of so many triumphs in the past. Prior to the race the newspapers quoted Stuart Barrett as saying he had Beasley riding regular work for him at his base in Portmarnock as well as on the racetrack and that his form was good and confidence was as high as it had ever been.

There was a good deal of talk in the specialist press in the lead up to the Leopardstown Chase that day, mainly concerning the forthcoming battle between Glencaraig Lady and the reigning Gold Cup holder L'Escargot, with many observers keen to see the outcome in order to allow them assess the horses' chances at Cheltenham in March.

Aside from those two, there was also considerable interest in the fact that Bobby had been given the ride on a horse called No Other in the same race, by no less a supporter than Lord Fingall, the owner of his 1959 Gold Cup winner Roddy Owen.

The race was won by 16/1 outsider Macroney, with Kings Sprite second and L'Escargot (who would go on to retain his Cheltenham crown less than a month later) third. Bobby was happy enough with No Other's fourth place, while Glencaraig

Lady's fifth was enough for most punters to rule her out of the reckoning for the Gold Cup. (They were right, although she would famously win the race in 1972 for Francis Flood.)

However, earlier on the Leopardstown card that day, Bobby had returned to the winners' enclosure for the first time in two years with a victory in the Stillorgan Hurdle on Norwegian Flag, trained by Paddy Murphy, to whom a big debt was being repaid by the grateful jockey.

'Two furlongs from home,' he would later recall, 'I thought that Norwegian Flag, on whom I was hard at work, had no chance until I looked at my rivals and realised they were doing no better than my chap. This was too good to be true. I picked him up, doubting there was anything left. To my surprise I found that there was. I wasn't the same man who rode those feeble finishes for Fred [Winter] two years ago. The old Beasley was back. I sat down and rode him out with all my strength. Three of us jumped the last hurdle upsides but I landed just in front.'

Tony O'Hehir remembers the occasion well, as it was big news in the racing world. 'I remember his comeback at Leopardstown vividly. He rode Norwegian Flag for Paddy Murphy. Francis Shortt had been the jockey and he was injured and Bobby got the ride. It was big news at the time because he had a big reputation, having won Grand Nationals and Gold Cups and whatever else and he was a big name in racing, not only here but across the pond as well. It was a surprise to many people that he did come back after everything he had been through.'

Bobby had, in the words of one journalist, ridden 'like a demon' to hold off two late challenges and to win to tumultuous applause. It was a fantastic start to his new career as a sober jockey, but one which demanded he follow a predictable routine, one that kept him away from temptation.

One person who was at Leopardstown that day and who recalls the enthusiastic reception Bobby got on his return to the winners' enclosure was his future wife Linda, who did not actually know him at that point.

'While Christy was very definitely Bobby's redemptive horse, the other one, of course, was his big comeback ride on Norwegian Flag at Leopardstown. I was there that day – I didn't know Bobby at the time or his story, to be honest – but there was a huge reaction from the crowd and I must say I was a little puzzled as to what was going on. It was a smallish race and I thought the reaction from the crowd was a little out of proportion. Obviously I quickly realised what it was all about. The crowd that day were truly effusive in their praise for him. He was a very strong pilot at his best, but he would probably maintain he was a long way from his best that day.'

Bobby himself maintained that the win was 'the psychological boost that I needed'. With that boost secured, Bobby now had a different challenge to face. 'But then, as for the rest of my career, there was no hanging about on the racecourse. I changed quickly, got into the car and drove straight home. On the way I went through a little town, which contained one of my favourite pubs at a crossroads. The [traffic] lights were red as I approached and I thought to myself that I could do with a gin and tonic. But, even as I slowed down, I was thinking "when those lights change to green, I'll drive on and I won't miss what I haven't had". The lights obliged as I had known they would. That was, oddly, one of the very few times I have ever been tempted. I am acutely conscious of the fact that I will always be only one drink away from hell.'

The reaction to Norwegian Flag winning the Five-Year-Old Stillorgan Maiden Hurdle by three-parts of a length ahead of The Grey Guy was unanimously enthusiastic. It was later described by then fellow jockey Michael 'Mouse' Morris as 'one of the greatest rides I have ever seen in my life'.

Michael O'Farrell, *The Irish Times'* racing correspondent, was positively ecstatic about Bobby's performance when writing in the following Monday's paper, 'What a race he rode to land Paddy Murphy's Norwegian Flag a narrow winner. Under pressure from fully three flights out, it took some driving on Beasley's part to keep the horse straight and up to his task.'

He also quoted Bobby as saying, 'He's a very game horse – I thought I had no chance coming into the straight. But he jumped great and should make a fine chaser.'

Bobby's ride on Norwegian Flag had been, in no small measure, down to the fact that Paddy Murphy's stable jockey, Francis Shortt, had been injured, but one of the first people to congratulate him in the winners' enclosure was the man whose misfortune had been to Bobby's benefit.

As the papers lauded the man 'surely taking a secure second lease on a great National Hunt career', Bobby's second coming continued apace with several more high-profile winners.

He rode Dim Wit to win the John Jameson Cup at the Punchestown Festival and it was said that 'few jockeys could have done such a good job in landing him the three length winner' in unfavourably fast going and that Bobby was now 'firmly re-established' in big race riding.

Indeed, in his report on that race O'Farrell said that for a while it looked like Peter Heron's Golden Emperor would win, but for the fact that Bobby – 'riding with all his old dash' – poached a length at the last and raced away on the run-in.

As the winners began to rack up, there followed a hat-trick of wins at Dundalk, Gowran and Tramore on Mick O'Toole's Alaska Fort. This particular winner would turn out to significant.

As the National Hunt season proper wound down –

Bobby amazingly finished fifth in the National Hunt Jockeys' Championship with twenty-one winners – and as summer racing got into gear, Bobby was still tipping away with winners at a variety of tracks and for a variety of trainers.

Of course, it was around this time that Captain Christy's racing career was just beginning, but it would be some time before his and Bobby's paths would cross.

★

The dawning of the 1971/2 season saw Bobby finding recognition once more in the UK, but in October that year he very nearly blotted his copybook in a curious incident where he got confused by the change to winter time from summer time and consequently missed a ride at Doncaster.

He had been engaged by Middleham trainer Peter Chisman to ride Ebony Prince in the Wills Premier Chase (Qualifier) in all the horse's races but he overlooked the swap from summer to winter flight time schedules and could not get to the racetrack on time. In his place Brian Fletcher picked up the spare ride and Ebony Prince won at 5/1. (Fletcher later and famously rode Red Rum to two of his three Grand National wins.) The performance prompted the trainer to comment that he felt the horse would one day make a Gold Cup prospect, making him a dreamer like the rest of us.

Despite this airport/timing glitch, Bobby continued to make good his comeback and rides such as the one on massive 17.3 hands high maiden chaser Ebony Lad – no relation to Ebony Prince – at Clonmel not only had the pundits grasping for superlatives, but also delighted the punters.

On that occasion – in the Sportsman's Novice Chase – Bobby showed he had lost none of his old guile when, having established a clear lead on his mount by the fourth fence, the horse appeared to make a terrible blunder and looked to have broken down as the jockey seemed to be pulling him up.

But there was nothing wrong with the horse and Bobby merely wanted to get a lead from some of the others in the race. Deirdre's Joy and Drumsill House duly obliged and Bobby tracked them until the third last when he once more assumed the lead and, when Deirdre's Joy fell at the second last, he was left alone in front.

He was chased down by fellow maiden Lockyersley and the two locked horns at the last with Bobby looking beaten. Nevertheless he summoned all his energy and, despite having gone half a length down, rode a driving finish to win by a head.

This and further big wins on such as Alaska Fort, Castleruddery and many others allowed 'The Skipper' (the nom de plume of the author of the 'Sporting Log' column in *The Irish Times*) to vent his fury at the aforementioned piece in an English paper which had condemned Bobby's return: 'The sequel was that the world famous rider who was so unsportingly abused, opened the new year by riding Ebony Lad to win Ireland's very first race of 1972 at Baldoyle on Saturday last.'

But something else was also happening at Baldoyle on 1 January 1972.

Christy and the Major

Captain Christy's racing career began at Limerick on 19 July 1971 in the colours of Mrs Tom Nicholson. Ridden by Tom Ryan in the Bruff Plate of £300 (£209 of which went to the winner), Christy faced rivals such as Denys A Smasher, ridden by Mouse Morris, and the eventual winner, Granstown Victor, ridden by John Kiely. Christy finished fourth at a starting price of 7/1.

'We knew the horse had potential,' John Nicholson said, adding that the aim that day was to give Christy an easy introduction to the racing game without damaging his fragile temperament. 'He ran better than we expected to finish fourth and, to be honest, we were delighted with him.'

His second outing came just a week later in the Lough Atalia Stakes over 2 miles 30 yards at the Ballybrit track in Galway on 26 July. This was not a big or important race in any shape or form – unless you were personally connected to one of the runners – but Christy was made the warm order 6/4 favourite and he justified the punters' faith by comfortably beating Master Val by eight lengths, again with Tom Ryan – or 'Red Tommy' as he was known – in the plate.

Reflecting on that victory, Ted Walsh feels that it was an

impressive performance by both horse and handler. 'He won his bumper in Galway – won it in a canter. That bumper was won by good horses over the years – Dawn Run won it – and it was always a race that fellas would lay out a good horse for. Tom Nicholson did that.'

Next up was the valuable Havasnack Plate at the Tralee Festival on 9 September which was the main event of the day. The meeting that year was notable for the number of outsiders to win the big races, and the big race on that Thursday was no exception. As it turned out the race was won by Ffrench Tune at 28/1 and the *Irish Press* reported the following day that the horse had been given an eye-catching ride by sixteen-year-old Colin Magnier, son of trainer Clem.

'Ffrench Tune won more impressively than the length verdict would indicate, for his rider never had to exert himself in the closing stages as Avondhu and Captain Christy were engaged in a neck and neck battle,' the paper said.

'In the struggle over the last two furlongs the 2/1 favourite Bagwanjia lost ground and never counted in the finish as Captain Christy, which had gone into the lead coming into the straight, was strongly tackled by Avondhu. Below the distance the issue looked to be confined to them, but on the inside rail Ffrench Tune, which had made up a lot of ground very steadily, went by effortlessly to win by a length.'

The Nicholsons had an opportunity to make up for the disappointment of Christy's defeat when their Articola was made favourite in the following Belvedere Two-Year-Old Handicap, but after charging through the tapes at the start, Articola was never a factor in the race itself, making it a very unsatisfactory day for the Kilkenny family.

It did not take long for Christy to put matters right, however. He was sent to the Listowel Festival on 29 September for the

2-mile Newcastlewest Plate and, having been napped by tipsters in several of the national papers, he was duly sent off the 4/5 favourite, again under Tom Ryan.

The following day Brian Featherstonehaugh in the *Irish Press* reported that 'one of the most promising young horses seen out for some time' is Mr Tom Nicholson's bargain buy Captain Christy which won the Newcastlewest Plate by twelve lengths. This, he added, made Christy available for handicapping in the Cesarewitch, a race which the Nicholson-trained Bigaroon had won the previous year and would win again in 1971. Following the Listowel victory though, Featherstonehaugh noted that whether or not Christy ran in the Cesarewitch 'the gelding has already proved a great Ballsbridge bargain for the owner'.

As it turned out, Christy did not go to the Cesarewitch and was instead aimed at the Prix Gladiateur over 3 miles at Longchamps on 24 October with flat champion Johnny Roe booked to ride.

Looking back over the horse's racing career Pat Murphy reckons the decision to send the horse to Paris to run the Prix de l'Arc de Triomphe meeting was an odd one.

'The Prix Gladiateur run was an interesting one because Christy had only run over two miles to that point, but suddenly here he was running over three in France. He was a young horse then and might have been too young for that,' he says.

'I travelled with the horse that time and when we arrived there the ground was very hard,' John Nicholson recalls, 'but [unknown to anyone outside the family] we actually had the horse sold before going to France and we were afraid he would break down because the going was so firm.

'Johnny Roe wanted to make the running on him because he felt he had no chance otherwise. My father said to him that he could not give those instructions as the horse had been sold.'

It turned out to be a prescient move as the ground in Paris that day was totally unsuitable for the horse. The four-year-old was in second place coming into the straight, but then dropped right back through the field, with Roe reporting later that 'the ground was all against him' and that 'he only started to run when meeting soft patches'. The connections were not terribly unhappy with the performance as Christy had not been hard-pressed by Roe since the jockey reasoned there was nothing to be gained by doing so.

It was then speculated that Christy would be seen next in the Naas November Handicap, but the Nicholsons were keeping their powder dry about 'a possibly lucrative career over hurdles this winter'. A 'stable spokesman' was reported as telling the media that 'we shall be taking it easy with him'.

In fact, the Nicholsons would not be doing anything – easy or otherwise – as he had already been sold.

The man who bought the horse was an expatriate Briton, Major Joe Pidcock, a career army man with a bit of racing experience who had inherited a large amount of money and had moved to Ireland. He had, he revealed to the Nicholsons, recently lost his mother but assumed control of the family money as a result of her will. And it would appear he was not afraid to spend it.

The Major was an eccentric character – allegedly, he once shot a horse which had run away on him and when asked why, responded 'That's an expensive saddle on him and I wanted it back' – although it was said that he was a very generous man to his friends.

Tony O'Hehir remembers a character that certainly did not immediately fit into the Irish racing milieu. 'I remember Pidcock turning up at the races wearing a sort of tweedy suit, except that the leg of the trousers only came to his knees – like you'd wear when you were a kid – and a pair of green knee socks to complete the ensemble with an elastic garter holding them up. It was a bizarre sight and in many ways he was a bizarre character,' he says.

Whatever about his eccentricity, the Major was nothing less than horse-mad and wanted a national hunt runner that he could have some fun with. In his endeavour to find such a beast, he had consulted Gareth Dooley, a neighbour near his home at Scarriff Lodge outside Cahir. Dooley, in turn, asked the advice of George Williams, who pointed the pair in the direction of the Mon Capitaine colt which had been bought by Tom Nicholson.

'Major Pidcock lived below in Cahir and had retired from the British Army,' John Nicholson remembers. 'He had a passion for racehorses and was very friendly with Gareth Dooley who used to train a few horses near where the Major lived. On Gareth's advice he came down one day in a little sports car to look at the horse. He wanted a good horse and he wanted to ride it himself – particularly as he had an ambition to ride at Cheltenham.

'Now he was not the best rider in the world, but he came down, saw the horse and we agreed a price of £10,000 for him, which I can tell you was a lot of money back then.

'I'll never forget it because when he was paying for the horse, he took a shopping basket out of the boot, the same sort of shopping basket a woman would have, and he took his cheque book out of the basket and wrote out a cheque for the full amount.

'My father gave him back £200 in cash in "luck money" as was always the case with such deals in Ireland, but the Major was quite taken aback and didn't want to take the money as he had no understanding of this whole "luck money" thing. My father told him he was not getting the horse unless he took the money.

'Shortly after, my father put £2,500 to the £10,000 and he bought 86 acres of farmland over in Borris-in-Ossory in County Laois and we still own that farm to this day – all because of Captain Christy.'

The horse was duly taken away from his home in Johnstown and the Major moved him to Gareth Dooley's small yard near Cahir, where he would be trained and cared for until he was moved to Pat Taaffe's yard the following summer.

Ted Walsh remembers the Major buying the horse, particularly so as his family was very friendly with Gareth Dooley.

'Gareth Dooley used to be an assistant to John T. Barry, a vet in Fermoy. Gareth started off in Fermoy as a veterinary assistant and while I am not sure how he made the connection with Major Pidcock, it ended up that he was going to train for him. Pidcock had built a house up in the Galtees, while Gareth was master of the Tipperary Foxhounds down there and lived outside New Inn. He also used to teach the kids out of Rockwell College – including the likes of Walter Swinburn and all the Magnier children – as well as hunting the hounds. But Gareth was not a trainer as such, his place was more of a riding school than anything so maybe that had something to do with the horse ultimately being moved on to Pat Taaffe.'

Whatever about that, there were those with misgivings about the Major's ability to extract the most from the horse. Ted Walsh was one.

'The Major paid ten grand for the horse – which was a hell of a lot of money back then – but the thing was that he was never really able to ride him. I remember Pidcock coming up here to my father with Gareth, who was a lifelong family friend of ours, and we brought the horse out to the Curragh to school. My father would go down there with a horse for them to go round with Christy. In fact, my father sold the Major a horse called The Innisfallon – an oul' horse he'd bought off Kevin Healy in Midleton. I'd won a chase on him and he was a safe oul' horse and just the thing for the Major who needed something to get a bit of practice on to keep him sharp for Captain Christy,' he says.

News of the sale did not become public knowledge until Christmas Eve 1971, when the *Irish Press* revealed that Captain Christy had been sold by Tom Nicholson. In its preview for the Limerick meeting on St Stephen's Day it noted that 'one of Ireland's top stayers' Captain Christy who 'had recently changed hands after being bought by Major Joe Pidcock from owner Tom Nicholson, makes his first hurdling appearance in the County Maiden Hurdle in Limerick and would need to jump only with moderate ability to score handsomely'.

Unfortunately it did not quite work out that way and *The Irish Times* subsequently reported that Christy was made 9/4 favourite for the contest 'but his supporters knew their fate early on, for he and Arcadian View, who were disputing the lead, ran out onto the chase course'. Both horses were duly disqualified.

Christy's breeder, George Williams, remembers the race and recalls that the jockey of Arcadian View, on the basis that the Major could afford a few bob, wanted him to pay the £25 he was fined because he would not have been fined had he not been carried onto the wrong course. The Major declined this offer and harsh words were exchanged between the two before one of the stewards intervened.

Pat Murphy reckons that the performance in Limerick that day was a fair indication of where the horse was – mentally – at that time.

'When he ran out at Limerick, that told you everything about Christy – he was capable of doing anything. He ended up at Pat Taaffe's at the right time in his life, but he had had a good education and won a couple of races. The thing was that the potential was there. Pat knew that, but to be fair there were plenty of people around Ireland at the time when Joe Pidcock had him, who thought that in the right hands this could be a good horse. But he just happened to end up with Pat at the right time. Any longer with Joe Pidcock and he'd never have been the horse he became. I think the "Galloping Major" was just about as nutty as the horse was,' he maintains.

Christy, of course, was known to be a headstrong beast and there are many who speculated at the time that while the sixty-year-old Major's intention had always been to ride his new purchase himself, perhaps he might have been better advised to allow a younger man do the job, even if he had ridden a few winners in his career.

Interestingly, especially in the light of the direction Christy's career would take, on the same day as the incident at Limerick, all the racing press reported on a fine victory by The Dikler in the King George VI Chase at Kempton, where he beat Spanish Steps and Titus Oates in what was described as 'one of the best finishes' ever seen in the race. Little did people know then that the novice horse who ran out at Limerick would eventually challenge The Dikler for some of the biggest prizes in racing.

★

Redemption was not long in coming for Captain Christy after the Limerick disaster and just a week later he appeared for the 1972 New Year's Day meeting at Baldoyle in Division 1 of The Sutton Maiden Hurdle, with Major Pidcock once more in the plate.

This was the day when the (future) legendary Irish handler Dermot Weld made his bow in the training ranks, scoring a remarkable debut double with Spanner and Chevy Chase.

Even that feat could not keep Christy out of the headlines, however, and Michael Fortune reported in the *Irish Press* that while Weld's achievement was greeted with great gusto, 'the most enthusiastic welcome for many that day was reserved for Captain Christy, the successful mount of Major Joe Pidcock in the Sutton Maiden Hurdle'.

Fortune further reported that 'this high class stayer on the flat was recently purchased by the Major and won in most impressive fashion in only his second run over hurdles'. In the wake of the one-and-a-half-length win over Marketing Manager and the 11/10 favourite The Met, speculation had it that Christy would now be aimed at Cheltenham.

On the same day *The Irish Times* claimed that 'one of the pleasurable highlights of Cheltenham next March will be the association of the now "62-year-old" Welshman, Major Joe Pidcock, and his £10,000 acquisition Captain Christy in one of the big hurdle events'.

Ultimately, this did not happen as Christy was sent to compete at the festival in one of the lesser races. But the paper reported that the reception accorded the Major in both the unsaddling enclosure and the weighroom, after he had ridden Captain Christy to victory in Division 1 of the Sutton Maiden Hurdle, was 'warm and effusive'.

'I did not like the horse at first, he was too difficult but I understand him now,' the paper quoted the Major as saying after his win.

The Irish Times also said that Major Pidcock lived near Cahir and had come to Ireland a year before. 'He has ridden sixteen winners in England, all pre-war,' it said.

The Nicholsons were in attendance at Baldoyle that day to see their former charge in action and John Nicholson says that they were quite taken by how well-behaved Christy was and also how well he jumped, although they were a little disconcerted by the Major's riding style.

'He jumped every hurdle in the middle and never kept on the rails at all and he told my father later that every time he saw a shadow coming to him, he flicked the reins at Christy and the horse responded every time. The thing was that he covered about a mile more than any other horse the same day, but he still won as he liked,' he says.

Ted Walsh was another interested observer and while it is fair to say that he was pleased for the Major and his new horse, he was not impressed with the jockey's skills.

'Pidcock was like The Duke of Alburquerque [a famous Spanish nobleman who loved to ride racehorses, but was not any good at it] or someone like that – a terrible jockey. He could not really ride at all. He had plenty of money and could afford to have horses, but he wasn't great at riding them,' he says.

'I remember the race he won in Baldoyle. He was in his sixties at that stage and even if he was in his forties you'd have said he was mad but as he was in his sixties he had to be stone mad. He used to drive a little two-seater sports car and I remember he drove my father to Baldoyle that day. My father got out of the car and announced that he'd been so scared on the trip from home, it was the last time he'd travel with the Major.' It would appear that some thought the Major to be every bit as bad a driver as he was a jockey.

As coincidence would have it, Bobby Beasley recorded the first winner of the New Year at the same Baldoyle meeting when he rode the promising chaser Ebony Lad to victory in the Portmarnock Chase.

If Cheltenham was the ultimate aim for Christy though, then there were a few more engagements to be faced beforehand. The first was in the Clane Hurdle in Naas on 29 January 1972 when the 'Galloping Major' (as he had now become labelled by the Irish papers) and Christy lined up against a strong field including Francis Flood's Perpol and Paddy Mullins' Brendon's Road, two horses he would meet again and again throughout his career.

Those two finished in first and second respectively and Christy was a distant – and very disappointing – fifth, once more prompting whispers that the Major was not up to the job. That said, however, there were those who admired his courage in taking on this particular challenge at his age. One such was veterinarian Jimmy Kelly who would later care for Christy throughout his career with Pat Taaffe. 'I saw Christy run at Naas once with Pidcock up on him and he was a brave man. He had balls, that's for sure,' he recalls succinctly, although he admitted that it was never likely the pair would be an item for very long.

Tos Taaffe was of the same opinion and he noted that 'the Major was more or less training Christy himself and he rode him a good few times too and even won on him', despite his lack of skill in the saddle.

Even though he lacked the necessary skills, Pidcock was once more in the plate for Christy's next outing in the very valuable Scalp Hurdle – then regarded as Ireland unofficial Champion Hurdle – at Leopardstown on 19 February. If there had been doubts about the Major's ability to handle the horse, they were at least temporarily silenced with a fine third place at a price of 20/1 against very experienced rivals Super Day, ridden by John Fowler, and Tommy Murphy's mount Noble Life. Confidence had been somewhat restored and Cheltenham beckoned.

On 15 March – the day when future rivals Bula and Pendil

won the Champion Hurdle and the Arkle Chase respectively – Christy was entered in the 3-mile Lloyds Bank Hurdle (now the World Hurdle or the Stayer's Hurdle, as it used to be known) where he was distinctly unfancied by the festival punters who rated him no better than a 50/1 chance. They were not far wrong as he once again gave the Major a torrid time of it, running wide all the way around and seriously compromising his chances in a race won by Parlour Moor with Christy in sixth.

Michael O'Farrell told his *Irish Times'* readers the following day that the Major's mount had 'run his usual good race' but gave away ground to his rivals by 'racing on the wide outside throughout', fighting his rider all the way.

Richard Pitman, who would later play a pivotal role in the Christy story, witnessed that first Cheltenham appearance by the Irish tearaway and it left a big impression on him.

'I remember seeing the horse being ridden around Cheltenham by Major Pidcock and he went wide around the outside – he nearly went into [local villages] Prestbury and Winchcombe, he ran so wide,' he recalls.

'Every scout in the country would have been after him straight away if it happened today. That really was an amazing performance and it was quite obvious then that he was a very good horse.'

Ted Walsh concurs, saying that the Major rode him at Cheltenham in that race specifically. 'He didn't ride him in any of the novice hurdles because he thought there would be too many runners. He could have ridden him in one of the novices', but he didn't. At Baldoyle, the hurdles were only five wide, so by staying on the outside he was not too bad. But when you get to Cheltenham the hurdles are twelve wide and he was still on the outside. But Christy still ran all right and he certainly was not tailed off or anything.'

But if Christy impressed many at Cheltenham, further good results were not coming along thick and fast.

Following another disappointing run in the Fingal Hurdle on 4 April, where he was sixth behind familiar opponents Good Review and Noble Life, it seemed the writing was on the wall for the partnership between the 'Galloping Major' and his headstrong steed. Pidcock was, by now, getting well and truly tired of having his arms pulled out of their sockets by the unruly beast. Also, at sixty-two years of age he was, in truth, possibly not up to the challenge any more.

Pat Taaffe's vet Jimmy Kelly would later maintain that it was obvious to most racing people that it was time for the Major to move on to other challenges. 'I suppose Major Pidcock had come to the realisation that Christy was a decent horse in his own way because in the end I think the Major knew the horse had more in him than he was going to be able to cope with. He was a big strong horse with a real mind of his own and he did need a more experienced man in the plate.'

This view is endorsed by Tos Taaffe, who says, 'I saw the Major ride Christy at Cheltenham and he rode round the outside all the way and he was not, to be honest, a very good jockey from what I saw. I would say that the Major never really got to grips with Christy at all; he would not have been able to handle such a headstrong brute.'

The pair would nevertheless had one more outing together, but things were changing fast for the two of them and a sequence of events was about to occur which would see the Major move the horse from Gareth Dooley's Cahir base to Pat Taaffe's yard at Alasty.

Tos Taaffe maintains that while Christy was obviously a very strong-willed horse – 'a brute' – he is not sure why Pidcock arrived at his brother's door. 'I don't know why the Major came to Pat with the horse – whether he was advised to do so or made up his own mind. Christy was very hard to hold and very hard to manage and the probability is that he was gone beyond it at that time.'

Ted Walsh recalls the occasion. 'Along the line he decided to move the horse to Pat Taaffe. I won't say he fell out with Gareth, but the horse moved to Alasty. I was very close to the story all along, and as Christy was very free with Pidcock, I tried to help by schooling the horse a few times on the Curragh. I was a bit younger then, but I was well able to handle him. He was a good ride, a bit quick, but a great horse. When he arrived in Pat's, the Major continued to ride him and won a few races on him. Some felt that, initially, the Major blamed Gareth for his shortcomings. He thought that somehow Gareth was at fault and that was why the horse came to Pat Taaffe. I think he thought that as well as sorting out the horse, he'd be able to sort out the jockey as well. He thought Pat, who was just retired as one of the greatest riders of all time, would be able to straighten him out too.'

But even as the horse was being moved to Pat Taaffe's, Ted Walsh reckoned something had happened with the Major. 'Somewhere along the line the Major got afraid of the horse and he wanted to sell,' he says. 'All he wanted was the ten grand he'd paid for him. Pat Taaffe had a couple of owners who could have bought him – Roy McNeill was anxious to buy him too – but it was Pat Samuel who bought him and had him in Jane Samuel's colours.'

And so it was that Pat Taaffe and one D. W. 'Pat' Samuel became central to the Captain Christy story and these men were two remarkable characters in a story already full of them.

The Trainer – A Legend in His Own Lifetime

Pat Taaffe's retirement from a race riding career, which was as legendary as the many horses he rode, came on a dank December afternoon at Fairyhouse as 1970 dawdled to a close.

It was 28 December, to be exact, and while the news did not exactly come as a complete surprise to racing insiders, particularly given the amount of punishment the forty-year-old's tall but wiry frame had taken in a twenty-three-year riding career, it was a surprise to his many fans. But, back in the days when the medical assistance available to jockeys was considerably more rudimentary than it now is, he had taken a terrible beating over an extended career and he knew instinctively it was time to hang up his boots.

His family were there too and daughter Olive clearly remembers the occasion. 'I remember his last race and we knew he was going to retire that day at Fairyhouse, where he rode Proud Tarquin. I was about ten or eleven. He had ridden the Grand National winner that year and also had three winners at Cheltenham, so he was going out at the top, which was what he had always said he'd do.'

Pat had ridden Proud Tarquin to win the RSA Chase that year, while also having success on Garrynagree in the Cathcart and Straight Fort in the Queen Mother Champion Chase. Of course, he also won the Grand National on the Fred Rimell-trained Gay Trip on Saturday 4 April that year as well, so his retirement came at a time when his name was still very much in the public eye.

'He retired in 1970 when he was forty years of age,' his son Tom recalls. 'He retired at Fairyhouse and everyone here at home knew it was going to happen. We as kids were brought there for the day, but all we wanted to do was get into the swinging boats and we didn't really give a damn about anything else. We always knew he was going to train. He was quite old when he gave up riding, particularly given the injuries he had sustained during his career, but he was always going to train,' he says.

The retirement announcement made front-page news across Ireland and the UK as Taaffe truly was a household name. His association with Arkle alone had seen to that, but he was also widely loved – inside and outside the sport – for his quiet and unassuming manner and his gentlemanly demeanour.

Born on 12 March 1930, Pat Taaffe was, like so many others in the sport, bred for the racing game. His father, Tom, trained horses from his base in Rathcoole, while his mother, Kitty, was the sister of another distinguished trainer, Barney Nugent. He was introduced to ponies practically before he could walk and was brought to the hunting field by the age of eight. At just ten years of age he received the Best Boy Rider U-11 award at the Dublin Horse Show.

While Arkle and Taaffe would become universally recognised as the greatest horse-and-rider combination ever to be seen in

National Hunt racing, Taaffe's career successes were based on rather more than just one horse. He won two Grand Nationals – on Vincent O'Brien's Quare Times in 1955 and Gay Trip in 1970 – as well as six Irish Grand Nationals, on Royal Approach, Umm, Zonda, Fortria, Arkle and Flyingbolt.

'This is my last day as a jockey,' he told the attendant Fairyhouse press when announcing his decision to quit riding, in his inimitable quiet, unflustered manner. 'I have decided to hand in my licence. I shall set up as a trainer sometime soon, but exactly when I cannot say now.' His final ride was on board Proud Tarquin – it fell.

By February the following year he had taken out his training licence and had eight horses in training at Alasty, the farm near Straffan in County Kildare he had bought years previously for the twin purposes of raising his young family and – ultimately – training horses.

And, in a curious twist – one of those stories that the sport of racing in particular is so capable of throwing up – it would later transpire that the man whose career was so indelibly linked with that of the great Arkle, was the very person who had broken his partner's ultimate rival. Tom Taaffe relates the story.

'My father actually broke Mill House. Mill House was down at Grandfather Taaffe's place – also Tom Taaffe – in Rathcoole and he came to get broken at Alasty. The horse was owned then by Tom Lawlor of Lawlor's Hotel in Naas and Tom had horses in training with the likes of Fulke Walwyn and he was a larger-than-life guy. When Mill House was broken and being sent back to Rathcoole, his foot went through the floor of the trailer and his left hind joint was completely down to the bone by the time they went to take him out. They initially thought they'd have to put him down, but they decided to patch it up and see what would happen. They knew he was a nice horse at this point, but they did not know if he had an engine or not. Allegedly he always had a big scar on it, but he still went on to do what he did.

'To have had Mill House and Arkle so closely associated with the one person is just unbelievable. Actually we now have two ponies for the kids and one is called Little Arkle and the other Little Mill House. Kicking King went to a show recently with the ponies and one of the guys there said to me, "Tom, isn't that remarkable, you've got Mill House, Arkle and Kicking King all in the same lorry!"'

Alasty was now, however, a training establishment and Tos Taaffe explains the layout of Alasty and the modus operandi of the trainer: 'He had about thirty boxes and about one hundred acres of a farm up there. He had his own gallops and his own schooling fences, some of which were quite tricky; so any horse that Pat trained had to be a hardy animal and would have to go through the mill. That was the way it always was with Pat. He did an awful lot of road work with the horses and when they came in off grass that was the best way to bring them on. He'd let them out in the paddocks then. Pat always had his own ideas and the horses had to respect that. He was not a conformist, as such – he had his own ideas.

'While he was very quick to adopt new ideas – or anything on the veterinary side which he thought would help – he always had his own ideas. He was a very strong-willed fellow as regards horses, but he was such a good horseman he could make a bad horse ordinary and possibly even an ordinary one good. If the horse didn't like the regime, it was moved on quickly.'

The facilities at Alasty were somewhat rudimentary at first, but they developed quickly as Pat invested in the place in order to bring it up to speed with the requirements of a modern racing yard. But not all the work was done on the farm's own land, as Olive explained, 'We worked the horses where my brother Tom [Taaffe] now is and the home place is about a mile and a half from there. The horses were always worked up what we then called Ted O'Connor's hill and he owned a big farm there. When that land was eventually sold it was broken up into different lots and Tom actually bought the land that my father used to train his horses on. We didn't own it at the time, but my father used the land with Ted's permission. In actual fact, my father's first winner was a horse called Russian Friend which Ted owned and which Ted Walsh rode to success.'

Her view is supported by the year's vet Jimmy Kelly. 'The facilities at Alasty were obviously adequate for the job, but they were not outstanding by any means. He did a lot of road work and you could not attempt to do it now with a string of horses. But he did plenty of slow work with them and never asked them to do anything until they were well fit. He must have soaked up a lot at Dreaper's [where he rode the great Arkle for the legendary trainer] because when he did go training himself, he had plenty of good horses in a relatively short period career – lots of winners. Romanogan, Roman Bar, Thartistle and so on.'

Pat Murphy, who had arrived at Alasty as a sixteen-year-old, was a wide-eyed young man from Hospital in County Limerick who had been an apprentice at Dermot Weld's. Dermot was only in the second year of what would become a legendary training career and Pat was getting heavy for riding on the flat. So Weld suggested he go to a 'mixed' yard and he thus ended up at Pat Taaffe's in early 1973. He recalls clearly the set-up at Alasty.

'He had a lovely yard and a good schooling ground. The gallops were fields – not necessarily all of which were Pat's and not necessarily all of which we had permission to go into. But we did gallop them and – I laugh every time I think about it – I can tell you that, great jockey he was, he was the most competitive man I ever rode work with. I've never, even to this day, seen anything like it. He did not like getting beaten in any shape or form, even on the gallops. And he was the one training the horses.

'But basically the gallops were on wet fields and stuff like that. Certainly the facilities were a little raw, but we sure got the results. He did an incredible amount of road work because around Alasty there were very good country lanes with very good hills. A lot of it was trotting – especially up the hills – and the great thing with Pat was that he would do an awful lot of groundwork with the horses to get them hard before they'd start doing any serious work at all. Once he got them fit – and also in between races – they'd spend an enormous amount of time on the roads. We'd do the road work and then we'd trot into someone's field.'

Pat's son Tom was only seven years old in 1970 and had been born and reared at Alasty which, he recalls of the time, had a lot of scope for development.

'My dad pretty much started training once he retired from riding and he developed the place slowly, putting up a few boxes here and a few more there as the years went on. In your early days as a trainer everyone will give you horses, especially the chancy fellas who don't really ever want to pay you, because they know they can catch you out as a new trainer. I fell into that trap myself in the early days. It is quite amazing the many small owners, or even older more respected guys, that will give you a horse on the basis that if you can train, well and good, and if you can't they won't pay.' This is a very pertinent point in relation to how Pat's training career would develop and it is something which still annoys Tom to this day.

'My father got caught by two people in particular who took him to the cleaners and it took me a long time to get them back,' he says. 'It took me a long time to square it with both of them. They left substantial debts behind them – a lot of dough. But I got the two of them back and I have to say it was something which had burned with me for a long time.'

But at this point Pat Taaffe was more concerned with developing himself as a trainer as well as the facilities at Alasty.

Describing the layout on the farm, Tom says, his father had very original hunting-type fences. 'He had a couple of them down by the river, two of which were small fences and then on the other side of the river there were three hurdling-type fences that led up into another fence and then, across the middle of the field, there was this horrible fly-fence with a two-and-a-half foot drop the other side of it. I was nearly killed off several horses there. My God, when I think back to the falls we got off horses at that fence. There was a free mare called Scottish Maid when I was about twelve or thirteen and I remember one day being told that she needed to learn and I was put up on her. She was going about a million miles an hour by the time she got to that flight. She took off at a terrific speed, but forgot completely about the landing part of it and she did a complete 180. I remember getting up off the ground – and I didn't even know what had happened – and being told: "We'll go back and do that again". I mean, with our own kids now, it is all about building confidence – not killing them. But that is how hard people of my father's era were. That's how they did things back in those days; it was very different from how it is now. We survived, though.'

Ted Walsh also remembers Alasty and the individual stamp Pat put on the place. 'In fairness to him the three fences at Alasty were unique. They were down by the bank of the river and there was not much distance between them and they were very narrow. And the thing was that there was a big hedge after that last fence and you just had to pull up.'

The transition from riding to training was a relatively seamless one but his family recalls that from the beginning there were expectations of success at the highest level. Pat's daughter Olive recalls that 'it was so normal' to have success at Cheltenham. They were used to it when Pat was riding and they now expected more from him as a trainer.

'I mean, if you look back at the stats., my father probably had a couple of winners there every year when we were children and he had twenty-five in all. And of course he won the Gold Cup four times as a jockey and, as kids, we sort of came to expect him to have success. It was just so normal in our house to have success there.

'My father's record at Cheltenham is incredible when you think that when he started there were only two days' racing at the festival, and then there were three and now there are four. It is easier now for jockey to pile up numbers there and it is incredible to think that my father won so many and his total has only just been surpassed by Ruby Walsh.'

Her view is echoed by her brother Tom. 'It's funny in a way because we were brought up in an atmosphere where winning the Gold Cup seemed no different from going out to get the paper. From the time you were able to understand, people were talking about winning Gold Cups and King Georges. When you think of it, 1964, '65 and '66 were all Gold Cups and then there was another in 1968 with Fort Leney, so winning another one in the early '70s didn't seem like it was any great surprise. That was my view as a kid, so the reality was a lot different. But that was how it seemed to me back then, because I certainly did not understand the enormity of the whole thing. We were just brought up in that environment where, when you went racing, you expected winners and when you went to Cheltenham you won a Gold Cup.'

The expectations of his children might have been one thing, but it was the same for their father. Having set Cheltenham alight for so many years as a jockey, Pat Taaffe now wanted to make his mark there as a trainer. It would not take long.

Initially Pat's charges went point-to-pointing and he told the press that his first runner under National Hunt rules was expected to run by the end of March. In fact, his first big acquisition as a trainer was the seven-year-old Beggar's Way on which he had won twice the previous year as a jockey and which was purchased out of Archie Watson's yard for Mr F. J. Quinn. The first winner from the yard, however, was the bay mare Russian Friend which was ridden to victory by one Mr T. M. Walsh in the Bishopscourt Cup Hunters' Chase at the Punchestown Festival on 28 April 1971. The 2/1 shot won by six lengths from Rich Cream II partnered by Mouse Morris.

Ironically, the headline over the report of that Punchestown meeting in *The Irish Times* the following day lauded one Bobby Beasley. 'Beasley's superb coaxing gets Dim Wit home in front' read the heading.

Beggar's Way subsequently won the Usher Cup at Kilbeggan on 1 June with Timmy Hyde in the plate – again at a price of 2/1 – and then reappeared at Bellewstown on 30 June with Ted Walsh riding, but could only finish fifth. The horse was then aimed at the following year's Thyestes Chase at Gowran, but failed by four lengths to beat Dim Wit in the 1972 renewal. He then was sent to the Scottish National at Ayr in April where he finished a close fourth, despite having been brought to a complete standstill by a mistake at the second last. Shortly after that he was purchased by Pat Samuel with the intention of being aimed at the Aintree Grand National.

In December 1972, Beggar's Way won the Conyngham Cup at Punchestown under Tom McCartan by six lengths, prompting Taaffe to say 'he jumps better and better the further he goes'.

By then, however, Captain Christy had already come into the yard and for the next three years would be the star turn and would give Pat Taaffe some of the highest highs he had ever experienced in the racing game.

In 1972, when his book *My Life – And Arkle's* was published, the closing lines quote Pat as saying 'And if I have one dream left, it's that I shall one day school and train an Arkle of my own. In all the whole wide world, I couldn't think of any gift more wonderful that that.'

He didn't know it at the time, but he had already found his own Arkle.

Pat Samuel – A Man with a Vision

The man who bought Christy to run in his wife's colours had, at this point, led a very interesting and varied life. A hugely successful businessman around the globe, he had drive, vision and talent – not unlike the animal he'd just bought from Major Joe Pidcock.

Pat Samuel was born in Auckland in 1925 into a well-to-do New Zealand family. Born D. W. Samuel, although even at this remove he is reluctant to comment on his real name, for some strange reason, he was always known as Pat. 'I've always been called Pat ever since I could talk,' he says. 'My brother was named Albert, but my mother always called him Peter – we must be an odd family I guess.'

He says his family were not wealthy, but they were well-off and horses were always a feature of his childhood.

'As a child there had always been horses around the place and both my mother and father rode regularly. I started riding with the Pakuranga Hunt when I was only nine or ten and I've been involved with horses pretty much all my life since.'

His formal schooling ended when he joined the New Zealand Air Force in 1941 at the tender age of sixteen. He was, he says, inspired by the same patriotic fervour that gripped every young male of his age at the outset of the Second World War and as soon as he was old enough to enlist, he did.

His spell in the army kicked off an event-filled life which would see him travel the world and end up in the most extraordinary places and doing the most extraordinary jobs. It was the beginning of a very long and often bumpy road for the young Samuel.

'I joined the Air Force when I was sixteen and when I was seventeen I was sent overseas and I came back in 1945. I was in the Pacific area – the Solomon Islands – in Bougainville. I was not aircrew, so I never really saw any action. We actually had a bit of fun on Bougainville. The Japanese really held two-thirds of the island for much of the time we were there and we just had a small bit – "we" being the Americans and the New Zealand Air Force.

'The Allies tried to starve the Japanese out of it because they stopped all the food ships coming to supply them. There were about 250,000 Japanese on the island at the time and we did have bits of excitement as our superior officers had us as the second line of defence. The Japanese attacked one night and they broke through the first line and we were all pulled out of bed and issued with ammunition for our rifles and we banged away at everything we saw that moved; probably caught a few Americans.

'Anyway, they eventually pulled back and the only other bit of excitement we had was with the crocodiles. That was that. I was there for nearly two years and then I went back to Auckland, where, as the war was winding down, I was asked with three other guys to tour through south-east Asia – Java mainly – to try and find our prisoners of war who had been held by the Japanese. Of course I said "yes" and we headed off, spending nearly two years trying to find them all – trying to determine what had happened to some of them. The information that the army here in New Zealand had was that there would be four of them in one camp and six in another and so on and so forth all across the region. We very seldom found the numbers we were expecting to find and in all we probably found only about half the men we set out to recover. We then got them home. When that was finished it was the end of my military career and I got out as fast as I could.'

Pat decided he wanted to travel and selected India as his first destination, but while he was at the immigration office, he met a friend of his who was looking for crew to sail a 34-foot ketch to America. Never one to dither over a decision, Pat signed on immediately. 'So, we sailed to America and took nearly eighteen months to do it as we stopped here and there,' he says. 'I arrived in the USA with thirty-two cents in my pocket and that was never going to get me very far and I was forced to sleep on a bench for a few nights. But I learned that they were playing polo out in Beverly Hills, so I hitch-hiked out there and I was lucky enough to meet the guy that ran it and he asked me if I had played polo. I told him I had played all my life and he said, "Well, maybe you'd like to play a couple of chukkas now." I hadn't any gear, but they supplied that and I got up on a horse and played for a while. Afterwards I came back into the clubhouse and went and had a shower. Later on a lady came by and handed me an envelope and I thought it was just a note telling me how to join the club. Because of that I didn't open it for a while, but when I did I got a hell of a surprise because there was a one hundred dollar bill inside. I thought "Hell, they've given me the wrong envelope".

'Anyway I eventually dragged up the courage to tell the guy that ran the place that they'd made a mistake. "Oh no," he said, "we always pay a hundred dollars for scratch games because we don't have enough players. Would you be able to play a bit more? Maybe three or four times a week?"'

Pat could not believe his luck, gushing, 'My God, I'll certainly do that.' He promptly drove back to town and that night was the last night he stayed in the 'hotel' in Pershing Square in downtown Los Angeles where he had been based.

'After that I lived very well on the polo money and got on very well. I secured a proper flat for myself in Beverly Hills – it was over a bar – and I remember being seduced there on a number of occasions by this seriously beautiful looking woman. I never found out exactly who she was, but I certainly enjoyed the experience,' he recalls.

A shock was on the way, however, as the polo season on the West Coast came to a halt and all the locals decamped to New York to play. The polo stopped completely for a couple of months and Pat was suddenly in danger of losing his new-found livelihood.

But salvation was in hand in the shape of the man who had taken him on in the first place – he asked him if he would manage the Beverly Hills Saddle Club.

'I ran that for six months until one day this guy walked into my office and asked if I was Pat Samuel. I said I was and he then introduced himself as being a Mr Dobrinsky from the Department of Immigration and said he was going to go and get a warrant for my arrest and subsequent deportation. I asked him why and he said it was because I was working there and had no visa or anything. I told him I was from New Zealand and learning American methods of handling horses. He said, "That's a good one."

'In any event I said, "Don't deport me, for God's sake. My father wouldn't like that." The immigration guy said he would give me the option of making a voluntary departure and if I did, then he'd do nothing more about it. I agreed – not having much real option – and he told me I'd have to get out within the next forty-eight hours. My options were a little limited and I thought I could go to Mexico and get a job training horses, but when I went to the Mexican consul I was told that they were not allowing Australians or New Zealanders in unless they could support themselves for two years. So that was that.

'When I got back to the office, Dobrinsky called and asked me when I was off to Mexico and I told him I'd probably have to go to Canada instead because they would not let me in to Mexico. As I was nominally a loyal British subject, I said to him I hoped to get into Canada.'

And that is what happened as Pat decamped to Vancouver, having befriended the immigration official at the Canadian Consulate in Los Angeles who, it transpired, was something of a sailing nut and was only too keen to hear about Pat's high seas adventures en route from New Zealand to the States. He duly sorted out the necessary paperwork and Pat was on his way.

Pat's first job in Canada came about after a chance meeting with the chairman of the local brewery in Vancouver, where he had shipped up. This man also owned the local baseball team and offered Pat the gig as assistant manager of the team. It did not, however, take Pat long to realise he did not like the working environment and he left. He then got an opportunity to learn the ropes in the lumber business at Fort George in northern British Columbia, but after a year of that he decided the lumber business 'was not for me'.

He returned to Vancouver and set up the Handley Cross Stables and also reactivated the sport of polo in the city. But the job, while very satisfying, was not producing much by way of income and Pat duly took another career path. This time, it would prove a lot more fruitful.

'After that, the first thing I did was get a job selling used cars because it was about the only job you could get with no qualifications while also producing decent income. After a while they made me the sales manager and then I was pirated away by the guy who had the Volvo franchise for Canada and I was made the sales manager of that operation. Then, however, the guy who had the franchise fell out with the factory and eventually had the franchise taken away from him, so they made me the bloody general manager. But I didn't think it would last long as I thought they would probably give the job to some Swede. But that didn't happen and eventually they made me the President and CEO of Volvo Canada. I built up a national dealer structure for them and then negotiated with the federal government for favourable terms to assemble foreign cars in Canada. I built an assembly plant for Volvo in Nova Scotia – the first foreign car assembly plant in North America.'

It is worth noting that such were Samuel's management skills that within one year he had the Nova Scotian workforce churning out vehicles which had the build quality that the Swedes demanded. This was 1963 and the establishment of Volvo's first North American assembly operation is still something that makes the Swedish company very proud.

In time though, Pat Samuel's vision for the automotive industry in Canada would change and he would begin looking to the east – Japan specifically – and to the future.

He visited Japan and came back very impressed. 'Then another group of individuals [a group of very influential local industrialists] got a hold of me and wanted me to start a Canadian automobile company because the only ones in Canada were American as well as the Swedish one. So I thought about how to do it and I came back to them saying I thought it was possible, but first of all they had to secure an imported car franchise so they could build up a dealer structure. You cannot start manufacturing cars unless you have dealers to sell them. They told me to go and find what I wanted and I went off and eventually ended up in Japan, where I quickly realised that these people would ultimately sweep the world.' He reported back to Canada, but was scoffed at when he outlined his findings.

'I knew the president of the Royal Bank of Canada and he quizzed me about the whole Japanese automobile thing, saying that his advisers were telling him it would never succeed because Japanese cars would never sell in North America. I told him it was going to be a major success. "You've got a reputation for being a very good banker," I told him, "but I don't think you're a very good automobile man. They will sweep the world." It was the same when I went to meetings of the Automobile Manufacturers' Association after I came back from Japan and they asked me to address them about what I thought of the industry there. I told them that within three to four years the Japanese would be second in the world in terms of volume sales and that within five years they'd be at the top. All those guys laughed at me; I could not even finish my speech. They thought it was the funniest thing they'd ever heard, but they were not laughing for long.

'I ended up getting the Toyota franchise for the whole of Canada and by 1965 we were selling cars. Obviously that did very well, but in the end the financiers had to withdraw for political reasons and I reluctantly assisted in selling the company to a consortium of Mitsui Bussan and Toyota. The company has been one of Canada's most successful automobile companies ever since.'

Despite his business success in Canada in the 1960s, Pat Samuel had not been involved in racing at all, even though he did get involved with showjumping and was even a senior horse show judge in America and Canada. Eventually, though, he realised that 'they had prize money for racing while there was very little for anything else', so he started getting involved with racehorses. That involvement would lead him and his family to Ireland and would eventually see Pat and his wife, Jane, owning one of the greatest National Hunt horses of all time.

'With my wife being Scottish and an accomplished horsewoman herself and with Ireland being such a horsey place, we decided it would be a good place to live and we bought a stud farm at Ballinakill near Adare in County Limerick which was, and I presume still is, a very nice place.'

The Samuels settled into Limerick, although Pat was by now spending more time in aeroplanes than he was on terra firma, jetting around the world following what was a bewildering range of business interests.

When he did have time to think about life in Ireland, however, he knew that he wanted to be involved in the National Hunt scene – and so too did his wife.

'I was always attracted to jump racing because I had been involved in hunting and showjumping so it was only natural for me – when I came to owning horses – that I had a jumper rather than a flat horse, even though I did have a few flat horses and even won the Caulfield Cup in Australia. I once bought a filly in Budapest and she won several important flat races in France before being sent hurdling,' he recalls.

Those around the racing scene at the time recall the Samuels as being a somewhat flamboyant couple, although some – Tom Taaffe, in particular – thought they were a curious pairing.

'Pat Samuel did a lot of business in London at the time and his name would have been around the place,' he says, 'but I assume that he had heard of my father because of his exploits with Arkle in the 1960s and that's how they got together. He was a very dapper kind of guy and even though I was very young I was always struck by his whole demeanour. He had a great way of carrying himself. Mind you, I could never understand Jane being with him.'

Pat Samuel's association with Pat Taaffe was indeed somewhat coincidental, but with the assertiveness he had developed in his business dealings, he decided fairly quickly that this was the man he wanted to train his string.

'I just met him at the races originally and I thought that, as he had been a helluva jockey, if I ever got a horse I'd give it to him,' he says. 'He had just started training and I gave Beggar's Way to him and he certainly got the most out of him, although the bastard should have won the Grand National one year when he fell into the ditch at Becher's Brook. I would have liked to win the National and I've had runners six or seven times, but they were never in the frame.'

But, if he never won the Grand National, consolation was at hand when Pat Taaffe persuaded him to buy Captain Christy.

Christy – A New Start

On 7 September 1972, now in Pat Taaffe's charge and about to become part of the Samuels' string, Christy made his opening appearance for the 1972/3 season in the Havasnack Plate, the race in which he had finished third the previous year. Although still owned and ridden by Major Pidcock at this point, the relationship between the two was in its death throes.

Tom Taaffe recounts how that might have happened. 'Christy was a headstrong brute. He was a very free horse and he was a handful for anyone – a real handful for anyone bar an accomplished rider. Major Pidcock did not exactly fit that bill, but he was a real sportsman and he wanted to try and wanted to do well. Full marks to him and he got real fun out of it. It was no matter that the horse once ran out on him or was unplaced or whatever; he still won on the horse and he had great fun with Christy. He achieved what he wanted with the horse. I do not know why Major Pidcock decided to sell the horse, but I would presume that when my father came up with someone willing to pay the price, he was simply willing to sell.'

Christy was such a presence – not to mention the Major – that it is not surprising that Tom can recount details of their collective presence, even though he was a mere tot at the time.

'I can't say that Christy immediately struck me, but I was impressed when he arrived behind a very flashy Range Rover in a very flashy trailer and I can tell you there were not many of them around in those days. I remember the Major arriving in his jodhpurs and tweeds. And then they unloaded Christy. I don't know why the Major came to Dad – I'm not sure of that part – but I can remember him arriving into the yard with the horse.'

Like many others he now feels that this handing-on of Christy to his father was a seminal moment, but he tempers the thought by reconciling the fact his dad was too much of a gent to tell the Major the facts of life about his riding style and the effect it was having on his charge.

'Certainly,' Tom says of Pidcock, 'his handling of the horse in the early days did not help; there is no doubt about that. The thing with my father was that he could never bring himself to tell the Major that he wasn't able to ride the horse. But, in the heel of the hunt, Pat Samuel was a lucky guy.'

Michael Fortune's preview of the Tralee race in the *Irish Press* predicted that Patent Slipper, trained by the late Paul Doyle should win this 'amateurs' Derby' even with the likes of Captain Christy, Vainard, Scrum and Anglo Argentinian in opposition. 'This will be a really tough test,' he predicted.

In the event Patent Slipper duly obliged under the late John Fowler, while Michael Grassick was second on Vainard. A moody Christy ran a 'nothing' race and was last.

George Williams recalls being asked by Pat Taaffe to walk the course with himself and the Major beforehand so the new trainer could issue suitable instructions. As the trio paced the track, the trainer told the Major that he should try and lay off the leaders initially and lie third coming into the home straight.

'Ride him out with hands and heels,' Pat Taaffe told him, 'and you'll fly past. You're a certainty to win, if you do that.'

The Major was not impressed. 'Now Mr Taaffe,' he replied stiffly, 'this is my horse and I shall ride him the way I like.' The outcome was far from what the trainer expected and after the dismal performance Pat Taaffe told the owner that if he wanted him to continue as trainer, then a professional jockey would have to be engaged. The Major was disinclined to take the advice and instead sold the horse.

The wisdom of hindsight being what it is, John Nicholson now says that his father would have bought the horse back if he had known the Major wanted to sell. He did not find out until it was too late, however.

A watching Pat Samuel was a little disconcerted that Pat Taaffe wanted him to pay £10,000 for this recalcitrant beast, but he coughed up eventually and presented the horse to his wife, Jane. It was a decision in some ways he would not regret – in others he would.

The New Zealander recalls that shortly after he and his family moved to Ireland he was introduced to Pat Taaffe and – pragmatic and consummate talent-spotter that he was – he quickly realised he was 'quite the best there was when it came to training' and said to him one day that he would not mind buying a horse.

'He replied that I was very fortunate as he had one at the yard which "he could not ride one side of" and the owners wanted £10,000 for him. I asked was he any good and Pat said he was. That horse was Beggar's Way and he did really well for us and would go on to win the Conyngham Cup at Punchestown – and would later on nearly win the bloody Grand National.

'Sometime later, Pat phoned me and said, "Listen, I've got an excellent opportunity for you." I asked what it was and he said he had a client who had a horse he could not handle and wanted to get out of him. He said that there was this old Englishman who had a horse with him and who didn't value the animal as much as he did. He told me he thought this was a hell of a horse and that he could probably organise a successful sale if I wanted to buy him. I told him to find out and he came back and reported that the owner had paid ten grand for him and could take the same to sell him. I told him the horse would want to be bloody good for that money. At the end of the conversation I said, "Oh by the way, what's his name?" Pat replied that the horse was called Captain Christy.'

Pat Taaffe had invited the prospective owner of the horse to see him run at the Tralee meeting and the two of them drove down to County Kerry rather full of expectations, but the day did not, as we have seen, turn out as either expected, even though Pat Samuel did end up buying the horse.

'He said he was running the horse on the flat in Tralee and he brought me along with him to see the horse run,' Pat Samuel recalls. 'It was not an auspicious occasion as Christy got left at the start and was well beaten in the race – in fact, he finished dead last, twenty lengths last! I said to Pat afterwards, "Jesus Christ, that was an awful performance. You want me to pay £10,000 for that bloody thing, for Christ's sake. He would not be much good at anything if he can't even beat a field of highway [New Zealand-speak for bumper] horses." But Pat was insistent that this would turn out to be a really good horse and told me to buy him. "He'll be a champion, that horse," Pat told me. I took him at his word and I bought him although I had no idea what a champion he would turn out to be. If I had been in any way a careful owner, I'd probably never have bought him.'

Pat Samuel, given his experience in the bloodstock world, had a good eye for a horse, but he still maintains that Christy was 'not a good-looking horse in conformation', but as it would turn out, he could certainly do the trick on the racecourse.

However, there were one or two domestic issues to clear up before the deal could be finalised.

'I had just bought another horse called Grand Canyon – who turned out to be the best horse of his type in the world – but my wife Jane said, "What, you're buying more horses?" So I told her that we would share him equally – I'd pay the bills and we'd run him in her colours. That was that.'

He maintains it was definitely the case that Pat Taaffe was unproven as a trainer at that point – although he was universally famous for having been Arkle's rider – but Christy's new owner felt, given his background, he should be a 'hell of a trainer'.

'On top of that I liked him because he was a nice guy and we got on well together. After he talked me into buying Beggar's Way and the horse did well I had the confidence in him to do well. My wife registered him [Christy] and put him in races under her sole name, but I paid the bills and I got the prize money.'

Whatever about the Samuels' domestic arrangements, one man who knew right from the start that he had a future superstar on his hands was Pat Taaffe. Jimmy Kelly, who was his vet back then and who still acts in the same capacity for Tom Taaffe, says that the first time the trainer and he discussed the horse, there was no doubting the enthusiasm that existed in Alasty for Christy.

'One outstanding thing that I remember was that shortly after Christy had arrived at Alasty, Pat pulled me aside one day and said, "You know, Jimmy, this is the best horse I've sat on since Arkle."'

Kelly was understandably taken aback by this pronouncement. 'That really was some statement, just a matter of weeks after the horse had come to him and I very distinctly remember him saying it to me. I know that he knew what he had on his hands, but I can remember him – plain as a pike shaft – saying to me that he thought the horse was the real thing.'

Pat Taaffe had also expressed similar thoughts to his brother Tos, who recalls that Pat certainly thought a fair bit of Christy. 'Pat rode him in work and obviously came to that conclusion fairly quickly. He was a very strong horse and Pat quickly came to the view that he had real potential. Pat Samuel had a few horses with Pat at the time and it was probably because of that, that he bought him.

'You cannot compare horses, but I have to say it surprised me when Pat said Christy was the best horse he'd ridden since Arkle. And when you consider that he also rode Flyingbolt, who is the second highest rated horse of all time behind Arkle, it was definitely a surprise for him to rate Christy so highly. Arkle was a very different proposition to Christy. Anyone could go into the box with Arkle and he wouldn't mind, but if you tried that with Christy he'd put his ears back and probably kick you or something.'

However, as the world would later find out, Pat Taaffe was not too far off the mark. All too often in the world of racing, trainers make the most extraordinary claims about horses in their charge, but that was never Pat Taaffe's way and if he was making claims about Christy's ability at this early stage of their relationship, then he said it only because it came from his heart. It was not a case that his heart ruled his head. What he felt in his heart was real – and his head agreed.

But if everyone at Alasty knew that Christy was good, they also swiftly found out about his wild side, as Pat Taaffe's daughter Olive indicates, 'I remember the stable he was in, but I was never any good at riding, so I don't have too much recall on what sort of a horse he was or anything. Having said that though, you couldn't but know that he was a bit of a lad and very much had a mind of his own. He was actually quite feisty and difficult. He was a mad genius, I suppose. You know what genius is like in a human; he was just an equine version.'

If Christy was a wayward sort, then in Pat Taaffe he had found a trainer who understood horses and knew what made them tick. Pat Murphy illustrates the point.

'One of the key things about Pat was his understanding of the animals. I remember Captain Christy and he was a nightmare, that horse. He was an absolute nightmare. And I don't think that Mrs Samuel ever appreciated how lucky she was, firstly, that she had Pat Taaffe training him. Pat rode that horse ninety per cent of the time at home. Secondly, she did not appreciate either that she had Bobby Beasley riding him. In Bobby she had a jockey who was cut from the same cloth as Pat Taaffe. They were both horsemen. Bobby was the outstanding horseman/jockey of his era and, like Pat, he was a great thinker about horses. It might not have looked to you or me that they were thinking about the horses, but they were. They worked horses out mentally and, believe me, Christy took a good bit of working out. I saw that horse doing things you could not believe horses could do and get away with. I can remember Pat walking him along the road on a long rein and just running his fingers through the horse's mane. Not pulling his mane, just running his fingers through it. All the time the horse's ears were going and all Pat was doing was keeping the horse's mind occupied. Believe you me, if that horse got bored you were in trouble. And it was those little things that counted.'

And if boredom could not be allowed on Christy's agenda, then they soon found out that he had worked out a few other things as well, as Tom Taaffe recalls.

'I remember that when the vet Jimmy Kelly used to drive into the yard in his white Renault 16, Christy used to have speed wobbles in his box. He knew Jimmy Kelly and he knew his car.'

From his vantage point in box number eight in the main yard, Christy was definitely king of the castle and although the trainer himself did most of the work with the horse, other lads in the yard were occasionally mounted up on Christy to school him over the tricky Alasty fences. Pat Murphy recalls one incident which caused much amusement for the trainer, but was not so much fun for him.

'Looking back now, it is a privilege to be able to say I schooled Christy, but the first time I did so was actually one of the most frightening moments of my life. He jumped the first fence really well, but at the second fence he stood so far off it he actually landed in front of it and took off again. And at the third fence, he clean jumped the wing with me. Now the wing was probably about two feet higher than the fence, but he cleared it – not a bother on him. And that was Christy. Pat thought it was quite funny because everything was all right afterwards, but it was actually a very frightening moment.'

The thing was, however, that Christy had struck it lucky by landing at Pat Taaffe's yard. Here he found a regime which was hard but fair, one which allowed for horses with brittle temperaments who nevertheless had a willingness and appetite for work and lots of it. This was definitely a spiritual home for him.

'If you took a horse like Christy and put him in the wrong hands, he'd have been a nothing horse,' Pat Murphy says. 'Major Pidcock, of course, had the horse originally and used to ride the horse himself and there is no doubt Christy got away with a lot in his young days. But I am a great believer that there are certain things that make a horse good – it's like baking a cake – but might not necessarily make all horses good. I have half an inkling myself, even this many years down the road, that if anyone had tried to straighten that horse out in his young days, he just might never have had the spirit that he had subsequently.'

The bond between the horse and the trainer was a strong one and it did not go unnoticed by the staff. They could hardly ignore it. 'We always knew where Pat was in the afternoons – he was in Christy's box grooming him,' Pat Murphy recalls. 'All you could hear from the box was "Ah, stand up now" or "Ah, don't be at that". Stuff like that and if you ever got down there and had a peep over the door, it was always a job to know who was in charge. I think Christy was in charge most of the time. That was what made that horse, I am absolutely sure of it. He would not have been the same horse if he was in the wrong hands. If someone had got up on him and tried to square him up and that kind of thing, they would have taken the spirit out of him. And that's why I say that the Samuels were so lucky to end up with two people – in Pat Taaffe and Bobby Beasley – who understood horses so well and instinctively knew the right thing to do with him.

'The Samuels had some very good horses and Pat Taaffe found them the best of all in Christy. There was one thing Pat had in that horse from day one and that was great faith. Huge faith. Here we had a trainer who still rode his horses every day, despite being retired. From day one he could see there was a huge amount of ability in this horse; he could also see there was a huge amount of character. But I think that never bothered him as he had dealt with many difficult horses in his career. There is no point putting any other slant on this. That horse was difficult; he had a mind of his own. He was like a juvenile delinquent who had to be steered in the right direction – not forced, not bullied, just steered. In Pat Taaffe and Bobby Beasley he had the two right men for that. He had a huge engine and lots and lots of willpower. But there were days when he decided that racing was not for him and one of those days happened at Tralee when Pat took Pat Samuel down to see him run and he finished last. That told you everything about Christy.

'The raw ability was outstanding. It often struck me even then – remember I'd just come from Dermot Weld's big flat yard and I had also spent time at P. P. Hogan's yard in Limerick while I was at school and he put plenty of good ones through his hands – how good he was. You might be doing a gallop on a horse you'd consider to be a good one and Christy would just leave you for dead. The sheer ability of him and the speed for a horse that stayed three and a quarter miles was incredible.'

From his vantage point, fellow trainer Tos Taaffe is still amazed at the phenomenon that Christy became.

'He was an amazing horse because Pat was hard on him early on, but the amount of runs he had didn't seem to affect him. I was associated with Vincent O'Brien earlier in my career and he was very definitely a "cotton wool" man in how he dealt with the horses. On the other hand, the Dreapers never really raced horses until they were about five, as a rule. But this horse got a fair bit of hardship.

'He had a heavy schedule, but that was the type of man Pat was – if he thought the horse was able for it at all, he'd have a go. Vincent O'Brien was completely different in that a horse could be left off for a whole year with just one race in mind – and he'd win that race. I rode for him for a few years and he had horses there that could win any race, but they'd only race when he wanted them to. He had an aim for them and that was it. In fairness to him, he nearly always pulled that off – nine times out of ten anyway. Pat's strategies were completely different – he

Bobby completed his 'Triple Crown' on board Fred Rimell's beautiful grey Nicolaus Silver in the 1961 Grand National with a flawless ride around Aintree. (Press Association)

Bobby and Nicolaus Silver pass the post at Aintree to win the Grand National. Their victory made front-page news throughout Ireland. (Press Association)

Bobby and Christy early in their fruitful partnership; a determined looking Bobby has a handful of rein and Christy looks primed to run. (Press Association)

Christy and Bobby on the way to the post at Thurles for the PZ Mower Chase. (Healy Racing Photographers)

Captain Christy with his trainer Pat Taaffe. (Tom Taaffe)

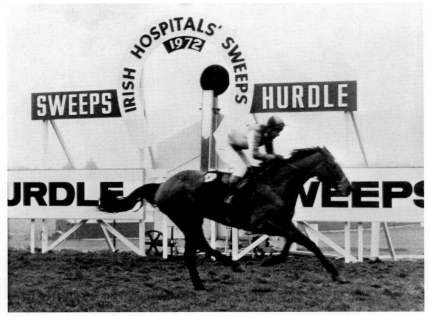

Bobby and Pat Taaffe shocked the racing establishment by winning the 1972 Irish Sweeps Hurdle on Captain Christy, beating the much-favoured English challenger, Bula, in the process. (Press Association)

A damp-looking Jane Samuel leads Christy and Bobby into the winner's enclosure at a sodden Leopardstown after his Sweeps Hurdle victory in 1972. Pat Taaffe follows in his sheepskin coat. (Press Association)

Mrs P.W. McGrath (left) presents the prizes for the Irish Sweeps Hurdle to Christy's owner, Jane Samuel, after his victory in the 1972 race. Pat Taaffe (second from right) looks delighted but Bobby less so – perhaps at the thought of receiving the Lismore Crystal decanter for the winning jockey. Also pictured is P.W. McGrath (middle), Chairman and Managing Director of the Irish Sweepstakes Organisation. (Press Association)

The Taaffe family pictured at home at Alasty around the time Captain Christy was making a name for Pat's yard (l–r): Peter, Carol, Olive (on pony), Joanna, Tom, Molly and Pat. (Tom Taaffe)

The moment Bobby was waiting for: Christy makes a blunder as he rises to take the last in the Gold Cup ahead of Ron Barry and The Dikler, but Bobby is alive to the situation and prepares to hold tight. (Mark Cranham)

The moment the dream nearly died: Christy has just barrelled through the last fence in the 1974 Gold Cup, but Bobby was ready for any mistake. The look of shock on many of the faces in the crowd tells its own story. (Press Association)

Bobby braces himself after Christy's near catastrophic blunder at the last in the Gold Cup, ready to pick the horse up for the dash to the line against The Dikler. (Press Association)

Pitching on landing, Christy nearly unseats Bobby, who finds himself desperately trying not to be flung out over Christy's head. Behind them, Ron Barry already has his whip in action as he winds The Dikler up for the run to the line. (Mark Cranham)

Bobby shakes the reins at Christy in a desperate attempt to make up for the mistake at the last as they head up Cheltenham's renowned finishing hill. (Mark Cranham)

Jane Samuel takes the reins to lead Bobby and Christy into the winner's enclosure at Cheltenham, 1974. (Press Association)

was unconventional in that way. He did his own thing and that was it,' says Tos.

'In many ways Christy was before his time. I mean look at the schedule of races he had over such a short period of time. These days the great chasers are put in cotton wool most of the time and they only appear every now and then; Kauto Star and Best Mate are good examples as they are aimed specifically at just one race every year. It was a fair testament to Pat and to Jimmy Kelly that they were able to keep Christy sound, given the amount of mileage he was clocking up.'

Pat Murphy admits that anyone looking at the schedule Christy undertook back then would probably be aghast, but he feels there was another angle to this element of the story.

'The difference between then and now is that horses seemed to be much healthier way back then. Nowadays we have got lots of viruses that affect the horses' chests and lungs and whether it is just the way they are stabled and the bedding that is used, or whether it is the atmosphere with all the different crops and all the different things they are sprayed with now, I cannot say. But back then there was not so much of that and particularly in that area. I cannot ever remember, in six years at Pat Taaffe's, his horses ever being unhealthy.

'When I think back to it now, I think that was key. It was easier to keep horses fit because they were healthy. The horses back then were also a different type of horse than those we see nowadays. They were much bigger and stronger individuals back then, but when Pat galloped one, it galloped. When those horses had worked, they knew they had worked. They did lots of cantering, but lots of road work in between. The thing with Pat was that he loved horses so much and he knew horses. He knew what every one of those horses could take. Pat Taaffe was a man who had done everything as a jockey – Gold Cups, Grand

Nationals, you name it. And he was a wonderful horseman and while some might say he was hard on horses, he was hard only in that they raced and they worked. But you know, I cannot ever remember any of the horses in that yard ever being unhealthy or unhappy.'

Whatever about the racing schedule or the demands made of the Alasty horses, Ted Walsh feels that over the years the stories about Christy's waywardness have got legs and become greatly exaggerated. He maintains that the horse was far from being a mad thing.

'Anyone trying to tell you that Christy was a mad horse is wrong,' he states firmly. 'Pidcock rode him and it is fair to say that Pidcock would not be safe in a car with the doors closed. Yet he rode Christy on a racecourse. A sixty-five-year-old that couldn't ride, could not have ridden a mad horse. Pidcock was no more than a passenger on Christy and any bad habits the horse got – he got them from the Major. Christy just liked to get on with things. Pat Taaffe used to ride him at home, but Pat was much younger and only just retired, so he had the strength to control him. The thing was that Christy was not mad; he just liked to get on with it.

'He was not particularly highly strung either. Pat got on well with the horse and he used to talk to him all the time. That was his way. He would not tie the horse up when he went into the box with him. Most horses in old-school places were always tied up when they were being done over – having coats groomed or their manes brushed. Pat never tied him up and the horse would be there walking around the box with Pat, going around after him to try and get the job done. That was his way. He was a very gentle man. Sure, he was a strong man and took no nonsense, but he would never abuse a horse. There was not a bad bone in him. He'd be in the box with Christy and he'd be talking away to him and the horse would be walking around. Christy was not a box walker or a weaver; he was a bit fussy, but that is all he was. He was always an easy horse to load into the horsebox and he would go anywhere.

'Pidcock rode him when the horse was at the height of his powers and if there was anything mad or bad about Christy he would have killed him. But he didn't. In the heel of the hunt, I believe, he was at worst fussy and that was down to Pidcock. He did have his own mind, but I never found him to be a bad egg. I remember Pidcock getting on him on the Curragh and they'd go a good gallop. Certainly he was not an armchair ride, but even Pidcock could ride him and if he could ride him, anyone could,' Walsh maintains.

Christy – A Star Emerges

C aptain Christy's first outing in his new owner's colours was in the Saggart Hurdle at Naas on 14 October when Tony Power in that morning's *Irish Press* opposed four-time winner Ballyowen in favour of Christy, but his optimism was not fully vindicated as the horse finished second to the favourite under Bobby Coonan, beaten by five lengths.

The following day's *Sunday Independent* recorded that Christy had found the going too fast for him and said that 'even before he took the second last hurdle out of the ground it was obvious he would make no impression on Ballyowen'.

Just a week later he was sent to the Curragh for the Irish Cesarewitch and was ridden by J. P. (Joe) Byrne who was claiming 7 lb and who worked in the yard at Alasty for Pat Taaffe. A 20/1 shot on the day, Christy was unplaced behind Phonsie O'Brien's Polar Fox, finishing ninth of twenty-four runners.

By now, however, the new owner/trainer pairing was preparing for Christy's campaign as a novice hurdler, but they needed a jockey. Fellow trainer Paddy Murphy had already urged Pat Taaffe to consider Bobby for riding duties. It would appear that Pat Taaffe did not need much persuading and felt that Bobby would be a good fit for his wayward charge. As Tony O'Hehir says, the pair would have been well known to each other, having 'ridden against one another back in the days and come up together as jockeys through the '50s and '60s'.

Pat Samuel doesn't remember there being much discussion about the matter, happy as he was to take Pat Taaffe's advice on most things to do with the horse.

'When it came to getting a jockey, Pat told me he'd like Bobby Beasley to ride the horse. I'd never heard of Bobby Beasley, mainly because I had not been around Ireland and England when he had been riding before. But Pat told me he was a hell of a rider and I was fine with that,' he recalls.

Pat Taaffe's daughter Olive says the matter was not addressed at home. 'I remember Bobby well,' she says, 'but his being selected as the jockey to ride Christy was something that would never have been discussed in front of us at the dinner table or anything. Other than that he would have ridden with my father and all the rest, but there was not much I knew about him then.'

She does speculate that her father could well have chosen Bobby as an act of mercy, as such a thing 'would certainly not have been beyond him because he was a law unto himself'.

'It may also have been that he chose Bobby for his horsemanship. My father was a real genius in his own way and he'd tell us stories about how – using a variety of tactics, be it holding a horse up or by taking an early lead, or whatever – he used to play with the heads of other jockeys to disrupt how they would ride any given race.' This, she suggests, might have been something her father felt Bobby was capable of too.

Her brother Tom has, at this remove, a similar take on things and feels that his father was happy to have Bobby ride Christy.

'You must remember that my father rode with Bobby and there was a sort of a bond between them – a friendship. Obviously my father was happy for Bobby to take the ride on the basis that he was a horseman and still had the natural ability to do the job. It may have been that the wider racing community viewed Bobby as a shaky character – and with good reason, you'd have to say – but both my father and Bobby quickly forged a great understanding of the horse and his character. They completely understood their two minds together going forward: that is one thing that is very clear. They both spoke the same language and whatever that language was, they were able to communicate it to the horse. I suppose you could say that they both spoke "horse" and it is funny when you hear people outside racing talking about people having "horse sense" but there is such a thing. They had it in spades.

'I never really heard my father talking about Bobby, because I was too young to be part of any such discussions or privy to them. I can remember Bobby being there for a cup of tea or coffee after he had ridden work. He didn't come down that often early on, but I remember the streaky straight hair. But he definitely spent a lot of time schooling the horse as that season progressed.'

For those in the yard the selection of Bobby as Christy's jockey was something of a surprise, but when they thought about it there was a lot to recommend the partnership, as Pat Murphy recalls: 'I suppose it is not something we see a lot of in the modern day, but when Pat engaged Bobby to ride Christy, it showed great loyalty to someone who had been a friend, someone who had been a work colleague and who had hit the worst time in his life, but always had the ability. Pat worked it out that if there was one man for one horse, then it was Bobby Beasley for Captain Christy. It was a huge leap of faith and I'm sure there had been conversations between them that I would not have been privy to, long before the decision was made. But I'm sure Bobby had straightened himself out and was looking to come back, but did not want to come back to be slogging around Limerick or wherever. He wanted to be at the big meetings and on good horses. I am assuming things here, of course, but the one thing I'd say about Pat Taaffe was that if I lived to be 150, I will never, ever come across such a genuine gentleman as Pat Taaffe. He was a person who saw the best in everybody until *they* proved otherwise – not Pat. That being the case, Pat would have thought that Bobby was once a great jockey and could still be a great jockey. That's how Pat would have thought about it. He would not have seen that Bobby had been an alcoholic and had blown everything he'd ever had – everything he'd ever put his hand on. He would simply have seen him as a great jockey. That's the sort of man he was. He was never a man who stood in judgement over anyone.'

This is a thought echoed by Ted Walsh, who maintains that Beasley was the 'ultimate': not only was he a great jockey, but he was also a brilliant horseman. 'Beasley was the Ruby Walsh of his era. He was everything and he'd ridden a Gold Cup winner on Roddy Owen, he'd ridden a Champion Hurdle winner on Another Flash and he'd ridden a Grand National winner on Nicolaus Silver. He had been reckoned to be the ultimate professional. As a jockey he had no flaws except in his head. Pat just wanted a good jockey and he admired Beasley's ability to ride. There were a few fellas around who were available for the ride, but none of the calibre of Beasley, to be honest. Pat was a bit eccentric in his own way and he saw nothing wrong with giving a fella a break. That was Pat.'

Having said that, however, he reckons that in the end Bobby was fortunate to have been paired up with Christy.

'Bobby and Christy were a great partnership, but for me Christy resurrected Beasley. Beasley was a great jockey – right up there with McCoy, Ruby, Martin Molony, any of them. In the late '50s and early '60s he was one of the best and even when he hit the bottle, he never lost his ability. He was always a great rider, very stylish. While he came back and rode winners, he might never have been heard of again had it not been for Captain Christy.'

Tos Taaffe concurs. 'It was because of Beasley's skills as a horseman that he got the ride. Bobby was a man with plenty of problems – particularly with his attitude. He was very stand-offish and he was a curious man. He certainly didn't trust many people and because of the alcohol, I don't think he even trusted himself. He was some horseman though.'

On 11 November, Christy went back to Pat's local track at Naas for the Rossmore Hurdle, where Bobby Beasley would officially take the ride on board Christy for the first time. Michael Fortune selected Home Chat to win the event and cited Christy as 'the main danger' and that's what he was – he won.

The Irish Times headlined the first win for the new pairing the following Monday and then quoted the jockey as saying, 'It's a long time since I sat on such a good lepper. I was impressed.'

He further commented that 'he's such a good jumper that he really needs a good, strong gallop which he did not get for the first half'.

Pat Taaffe said afterwards that Christy was 'a very good horse and he may run in the Berkshire Hurdle at Newbury, but he's so well we will let him take his chance again in a hurdle next week'.

Now, in modern times, there are trainers who will tell you that horses need to be 'cotton-balled' and saved for specific targets. But that was not Pat Taaffe's way and it was not the Samuels' either.

'Sure, I take my hat off to Henrietta Knight the way she trained Best Mate to win three Gold Cups off the back of very few runs,' says Pat Murphy, adding, 'especially when you think back on the fact that Christy had had maybe twenty-five races – bumpers, hurdles, novice chases and so on – before he went to the Gold Cup. But that was the great thing about him because he learned from his racing and racing didn't take anything out of him. I think too that he pulled himself up in a number of races, where he should have known better, told you exactly how he was.'

Ted Walsh has a slightly different take on the amount of times Christy was sent out.

'He was one of those horses that you just couldn't get to the bottom of. He was a horse that followed no rules. He was a freaky horse,' he says.

'He was a hardy bastard, that's for sure. He put up with a lot of hardship. He definitely had a great constitution and you can say what you like about him but if he was a real worrier, then he would not have survived as long as he did. Plain and simple, he would not have come through it. Lots of horses sweat and fret, but it doesn't take that much out of them.'

And so it was that a week after his run at Naas – and in keeping with the Samuels' desire to see their horse run often – Christy was sent to Leopardstown for the Sandymount Hurdle and this time around Michael Fortune tipped him to win, saying, 'There was a lot to like about his win over Scrum and Home Chat.'

In the papers the next Monday morning all the plaudits from the meeting were taken by Johnny Roe who had secured his seventh flat jockeys' title on the day. But it was noted in the *Irish Press* that Brian Lusk's Mr Barcock, which had won the November Handicap, would be aimed at the Sweeps Hurdle in

December, as would Captain Christy 'the comfortable winner of the Sandymount Hurdle'.

In *The Irish Times*, however, Bobby found voice for a controversial opinion when he said after the victory that he now wanted to take on dual Champion Hurdle winner Bula with his new mount. 'They don't go fast enough over here [in Ireland],' he reasoned.

'Beasley may well get his wish in the Sweeps Hurdle here at Christmas,' Michael O'Farrell opined, adding that 'Pat Taaffe would be quite keen to run the horse in the big race if, in the meantime, he does well in the Benson and Hedges Hurdle at Fairyhouse on the ninth of next month'.

With some considerable degree of foresight, something not often found wanting in the Irish racing press corps, O'Farrell also speculated that Christy had 'tremendous potential' and 'could well develop into a leading Champion Hurdle candidate'.

Christy did not make it to Fairyhouse for the Benson and Hedges on 9 December because the going was too firm and several racing journalists expressed disappointment, not least O'Farrell who said that in Christy's absence the race had lost much of its lustre as he was 'surely the best Champion Hurdle potential we have had since Another Flash'. Reading this, Bobby must have had the chills.

In the run-up to the Sweeps Hurdle, however, there were few hacks willing to oppose Bula who was the class horse in a field which would include Fred Rimell's Comedy Of Errors, Paddy Mullins' Brendon's Road, True Luck and the American-bred Inkslinger, as well as Christy. There were those, however, who felt that if the tactics could be properly sorted, there was a chance of an Irish victory.

In his pre-Christmas preview in the *Sunday Independent* on 24 December, Tom McGinty noted that Christy was the 'most interesting' Irish contender in the big race the following Wednesday as, since joining the Taaffe stable and being bought by the Samuels, he had really flourished.

'He may not have beaten anything of great account in his two recent victories, but no hurdler in the country jumps better. He has seemingly bottomless reserves of stamina and there is about him that little something that so often gives the potentially great horse a sense of presence. Captain Christy will surely make a top class chaser one of these days, but a really good gallop under conditions that would prove a real test of stamina might enable him to topple Bula,' McGinty said.

In saying as much, he also reasoned that Christy was 'an attractive each-way bet' in what promised to be 'the best international hurdle race ever staged in this country'.

Tony Power, in his preview in the *Irish Press* also underlined the stamina factor. 'The "big gun" in the armoury of the two major Irish hopes, Brendon's Road and Captain Christy, is stamina,' he said, while also predicting that both horses would need a good strong gallop all the way to be totally effective even though it was 'sobering to note' that both had been 'knocking around in conditions maidens' when Bula had won two Champion Hurdles.

'Captain Christy has the advantage of being ridden by Bobby Beasley who is the only jockey in the race apart from Paul Kelleway [Bula's rider] to have ridden a Champion Hurdle winner. Beasley's experience at championship level and his rapport with Captain Christy can be decisive factors. It is also in their favour that they are course and distance winners,' Power wrote. He also warned his readers that while Christy had beaten Lough Inagh last time out, he had done so despite making a mistake at the final flight of hurdles. 'This afternoon he cannot afford to make any jumping errors anywhere through the race and, more particularly, at the last,' he maintained.

Despite the strength of the field lining up against Christy on Wednesday 27 December, Bobby and Pat Taaffe had been around the block enough times to know when they had something good on their hands and they were determined to make the most of Christy's stamina. On the Tuesday night before the race the pair sat down and discussed potential strategies. Bobby was confident he had the horse to beat Bula and both he and the trainer agreed that if Bula was to be beaten, they had to ensure the English raider would have too much to do in the last half mile.

They gambled on the fact that Kelleway, who in the past had invariably held Bula up for a killer late run in order to cut down his opposition, would adopt the same tactics again. The plan, therefore, was that in the soft conditions at Leopardstown, Bobby would pick his moment to slip into a clear lead, steal quietly away and build up an advantage that would be impossible for Kelleway to claw back.

'I told Pat,' Bobby revealed later, 'there's only one chance we have here and that's to jump off and go like hell. When we get over on the far side in the back straight with about a mile to go, I'll try and slip the field. Knowing that Paul will probably want to come with a late run and get through on the inside, I'm fairly happy.'

For Bobby personally, this race would be a defining moment. Even if he had been given an easy ride by the press on his return to the weighroom, with little mention made of the havoc alcohol had wreaked on him and his family, there were plenty of naysayers around who wanted to see him fail. His delicate sensibilities were heightened by the fact he knew this was the time to shut the doubters up.

There were obvious nerves in the parade ring before the

race as Bobby and Pat Taaffe readied Christy for the challenge ahead. There were few words between the two men and the trainer felt no need to issue any last-minute instructions to his jockey. The plan was already laid and there was no need for any final tweaks. That being the case, Bobby would later say he had cantered the horse down to the start 'with a confidence I hadn't felt for years'.

A youthful Tom Taaffe accompanied the horse to the races and remembers the day vividly.

'The Sweeps Hurdle was a great day. I went to Leopardstown in the lorry – one of those old CIE boxes that they used to use back then. Joe Fagan was the driver – an old man who used to smoke constantly – and an old board used to be put over the engine so us kids could sit on it. It was a very wet day . . . I was at the horse care end of it – saddling him up and leading him around the ring and that kind of thing.'

A record crowd packed Leopardstown that day despite desperately inclement weather, expectant that Ireland's 'new Arkle' could defeat the great dual champion. There was genuine hope among the Irish racing public that Christy truly was an animal that could gladden their hearts and fill their pockets in the same way that Tom Dreaper's legendary charge had.

The race itself unfolded in a fairly uneventful fashion until the fourth last flight, when Bobby picked his moment. As they cleared the hurdle Christy was full of running and Bobby kicked him on, snatching the lead from Inkslinger and the mare Super Day. Indeed, Super Day was another part of the plan because the two horses had schooled the previous Monday and Christy had reportedly 'galloped all over her'.

Bobby later commented that when he saw Inkslinger and Super Day together going to the fourth last, he thought it was about time he went on.

'Christy pinged the hurdle to land in the front on the inner,' he said. 'From there I motored on as fast as I could without extending the horse. Entering the straight I showed him the whip to keep him hard at work and I kept expecting Paul Kelleway and Bula to come at me. That was why I kept Christy just under full extension to have a bit ready when Bula came. I looked back after the last, though, and I could not believe it – there was absolutely nothing in striking distance.'

The pair ran out 15/2 winners of the Sweeps Hurdle by a margin of six lengths over Comedy Of Errors, with Brendon's Road a further length behind and a struggling Bula a further six lengths back in fourth. *The Irish Times* described it as a 'catch-as-catch-can' victory orchestrated by 'that masterful tactical rider Bobby Beasley' and said that 'the budding young Arkle had made an absolute procession of the race'.

Speaking to the racing press afterwards Bobby lauded Christy as 'the best hurdler I have ever ridden' and he added that he was 'a better stayer than my Champion Hurdle winner Another Flash, who was a brilliant horse'.

A 'thrilled' Jane Samuel said later that there had been no hard-luck stories in the race and she warned that 'if Pat [Taaffe] says he will win at Cheltenham, then you can take it as gospel'.

For his part Paul Kelleway was very magnanimous in defeat, admitting he had fallen into the trap which had been laid for him. 'I have no excuses,' he said, 'Bula was cruising at the fourth last. He pinged it and passed a few in the air, but from there he gave me nothing.'

Nevertheless, his further assertion that 'maybe this race-course does not suit him, as Cheltenham is really his course' found little favour with the Irish – and particularly with Bobby, who described the claim as 'ridiculous'.

He maintained that the English were still underestimating

Christy when they predicted that Bula would turn the tables at Cheltenham in March.

In his own quiet way, Pat Taaffe accepted the plaudits of victory with magnanimity while knowing full well that Bobby and himself had hatched a plan which they had pulled off in considerable style. Fred Winter extended his congratulations saying, 'Well done, Pat. I'll see you in Cheltenham. We'll meet again on my ground. Naturally I am disappointed.'

The considered opinion – among the bookies as well as Bula's English supporters – was that their horse would regain his form come the Champion Hurdle and that was reflected in the prices being quoted for the two horses in the March renewal. At one time Bula had been offered odds-on but now was listed at 5/4, while Christy, despite his convincing Leopardstown win, was a generous 4/1. The continued confidence in Bula was underlined by comments made by Comedy Of Errors' jockey Bill Smith, who said that while the 1972 Sweeps Hurdle had been a much better race than the one he had won the previous year on Kelame, he still did not know 'if Captain Christy would beat Bula at Cheltenham as Paul's horse is a different one there to anywhere else'. The arguments between the sides would rage all the way to Prestbury Park.

There was, of course, a savage undertow to the Leopardstown victory. Bobby – having deserted the fold, blind drunk – had now seriously dumped on his former employer. It was silently and maturely accepted by both. The only thing was that Fred did not have as much luggage to carry home.

For Pat Taaffe's nascent training operation, scoring a big success like this was very important and his daughter Olive recalls that 'while Captain Christy came along very quickly for my father, when he won the Sweeps Hurdle at Christmas in 1972, it was a very big deal. It absolutely lashed on that day in

Leopardstown and I'll never forget it, although we didn't really care once he won.'

Her brother Tom agrees. 'The media made a big thing of it at the time, but that was only natural given the importance of the race on the calendar then.'

If there was a relative media frenzy surrounding Christy's Sweeps Hurdle win, then Bobby too came in for a large dollop of favourable comment, although many people were still either unaware of or unwilling to write publicly about his alcoholism. A typical observation illustrating this point came in the *Sunday Independent* after the victory when Tom McGinty, reflecting on the race, commented that regular racegoers did not need the evidence of the Sweeps Hurdle win to tell them that Bobby was as good a jockey as he ever had been.

'It was, however, part of the thrill of the Sweeps Hurdle to see this accomplished horseman make the point in front of an international audience, many of whom had written him off even before he retired temporarily a few years ago following a crushing fall that not only kept him inactive for a long spell but also brought about weight problems,' he noted, studiously ignoring Bobby's drinking.

For the jockey himself the Sweeps Hurdle provided as many problems as it did plaudits and Bobby remembers having to be very focussed. There could be no elation because this would only lead to celebration and that meant temptation to drink. He recalled coming back into the winners' enclosure and being greeted by another trainer who shouted 'Well done, Bobby! That's the stuff.' The jockey's reaction was not what one might have thought. 'He had been one of my worst detractors and had never lifted a finger to help me when I was down. The two-faced bastard! Forget it. No resentment. Anger only leads to drink.'

He had earned his first serious bit of money in quite some time as a result of the victory and was already planning to spend part of it on a new cowshed for the farm in Wexford, but the drive home from Leopardstown that day brought on a sense of melancholia. 'It is a sad reflection on my home country that in most of those funny little towns every other building seems to be a chemist, a betting shop or a pub. As I drove through one of those towns, I saw a pub I had known very well from the old days. Two years earlier I would have stopped there for sure. Now I wasn't tempted at all. I thought again of the tragedy of Ireland's vast increase in alcoholism,' he said.

That despondency was tempered by the manner in which his horse had performed and on that long, lonely road home, he relived the race. 'I was already looking at it objectively,' he said, 'planning for the future. Captain Christy was clearly better than Pat and I had thought. We must be real champions. I believed that even if we had not outmanoeuvred Paul Kelleway, we would still have beaten Bula, winner of two Champion Hurdles.'

In any event, despite having an entry for his horse in the Schweppes Hurdle at Newbury, Pat Taaffe decided that the Scalp Hurdle at Leopardstown would be Christy's next engagement. It was 'a more attractive race' and both he and Bobby were being named that week's *Irish Independent*'s 'Sports Personalities of the Week' – 'primarily as a tribute to two great racing personalities' – and so the plans for the Cheltenham challenge were being honed at Alasty.

In the run-up to the race, *The Irish Times* of 14 February carried an interesting assessment of both horse and jockey: 'Rarely enthusiastic about the horses he is associated with, Bobby Beasley makes a notable exception in his Sweeps Hurdle mount Captain Christy who takes in the Scalp Hurdle on Saturday as a stepping stone to the Champion Hurdle. Having ridden Captain Christy after racing at Punchestown last Saturday, Beasley said, "He has definitely improved. He almost spoils me for other horses. It's like getting out of a Rolls Royce to drive a Mini.'"

In a relatively bloodless fifteen-length victory over Brendon's Road on 17 February, there were, however, some concerns about Christy's jumping and Bobby said later that his mount had 'lost the rest [of the field], despite some untidy jumping'.

Dave Baker in the following week's *Irish Field* described the Scalp victory as 'a most spectacular affair', adding that Christy had taken up the running from flag-fall and 'galloped his rivals into the ground' to hand out a thorough beating to Brendon's Road and Polar Fox.

Baker did note that Christy's jumping was not in any way flawless, commenting, 'He fairly flew his hurdles but was at risk at several of them, particularly the last, which he flattened.'

Michael O'Farrell in *The Irish Times* reckoned that, provided the horse got soft ground and a good gallop at Cheltenham, he was satisfied Captain Christy could win the Champion Hurdle.

He did say, though, that Christy had not jumped well in the Scalp and this was a worry. 'His jumping was not good, he hit several and took the last by the roots, but as rider Bobby Beasley said later, "He thought he was only schooling out there on his own and he got bored. He is such an intelligent fellow he just does what he likes. He moves much better on softer ground – as he did when schooled at Punchestown recently. I think he will take all the beating at Cheltenham.'"

Reflecting on it now, Pat Murphy reckons that the Scalp Hurdle was a race Christy won easily. 'To be fair, he had not run since the Sweeps Hurdle and going into the race he was already the great hope of all of Ireland as a potential Champion Hurdle winner. When he won it, he looked like a Champion

Hurdle winner waiting to happen. There were probably only two people thinking further than that at the time – Pat Taaffe and Bobby. They were thinking more along the lines of a Gold Cup. In fact, I don't think Pat ever truly thought Christy was a Champion Hurdle horse. Bobby too, especially having ridden all those great Paddy Sleator hurdlers in the past.'

Whatever was going through their minds and even despite the concerns about his jumping, Christy's price shortened dramatically for the Champion Hurdle as a result of his Scalp victory with Irish bookie Terry Rogers quoting him at just 7/4, obviously reflecting the weight of expectation – and money – that was now resting on Christy's broad shoulders.

The run-up to Cheltenham back then was not in any way as frenzied as it is now and all those preview nights were still many years away, but there was still plenty to exercise the minds of the Irish in advance of the festival. For Pat Taaffe and Bobby the focus was on the premier hurdle event and it might seem strange to recount now that their thinking led them to believe that it would not be Bula who would trouble them, but the horse that had finished second in the Sweeps Hurdle.

They dreamed many dreams in the weeks prior to the Champion Hurdle on 13 March and so too, obviously, did many others, as Christy's price kept shortening in the build-up to the race. Writing in his festival preview in the *Irish Field*, Dave Baker reported that while Bobby Beasley was very confident of Captain Christy's chances, this was a view to which he too subscribed.

'Captain Christy went on to win at Leopardstown last month and although far from foot perfect, never seemed in danger of falling in a round which was full of exuberance and at times breathtaking jumping.' He predicted more of the same at Cheltenham.

But it was not to be.

Pat Murphy reckons that before the race, Christy was being prepared more in hope than expectation.

'But the thing about Pat and Bobby was that they had been there and done it before, while nobody else in the yard had. Even though the horse nearly ended up as favourite for the race, there was reasonable expectation. I can almost remember Pat saying to the farrier, "He'll be third or fourth." He felt that the top two English horses might have more pace coming down the hill.'

Christy had been to Cheltenham the previous year and had taken the trip over to England in his stride. This time around it was very different and he fretted and sweated throughout the journey. Bobby, who accompanied him in the horsebox, reckoned the horse 'must have lost half a hundredweight on the way over'. He knew this would obviously have a very detrimental effect on the horse's chances on the big day, but the news did not leak out and the punters kept their faith.

Christy was sent off the favourite at the unusual price of 85/40, even though the connections were worried about the effect the journey had had. However, it would turn out that Bobby and Pat Taaffe were not quite as on the ball, especially considering the horse's potential fitness, as they had been in the Sweeps Hurdle when it came to the tactics they employed.

When the tapes went up it was Easby Abbey that took up the pacemaking duties, which were moderate at best and, as the field came down the hill Bobby realised the error of judgement and knew the pace was not anywhere near strong enough. With only two flights of hurdles left, the jockey realised he had a sprint on his hands and so the race fell to Comedy Of Errors, who was by the sprinter Comedy Star, who won by one and a half lengths from Easby Abbey with Christy a further two lengths away. Four lengths covered the first six horses home.

A disgruntled Bobby was quoted as saying, 'We tried new tactics and held him up. If we'd let him make the running as he liked he would have won.' Oddly enough, these new tactics would later prove to be the making of Christy.

Michael O'Farrell reported the following day in *The Irish Times* that 'the writing was on the wall for Captain Christy when his jockey Bobby Beasley failed to get the necessary response from his mount coming down the hill in yesterday's Champion Hurdle. The race was won fairly and squarely by Sweeps Hurdle runner-up Comedy Of Errors – the only horse feared by Beasley and Pat Taaffe.'

He added, somewhat fatuously, that 'the ground was not soft enough for the Captain but I am pleased, for he ran a grand race'.

Both Beasley and Taaffe told the attendant media that despite their disappointment with the outcome, the result was possibly the best thing for the horse because if he had won they would have had to stick with him over hurdles, but now they could comfortably move forward to the chasing game, which both felt was his true forte.

Interestingly, Pat Samuel now says that these fears were completely unfounded as he too wanted to see Christy join the chasing ranks. 'I don't think that was the case for a minute, because I was quite prepared to see him go on and start chasing.'

It is worth noting that two days after Christy's disappointing performance in the Champion Hurdle, The Dikler and Pendil fought out a tight finish in the Gold Cup with The Dikler winning by a head.

Both would be on Christy's radar a year later.

★

Christy did gain some measure of compensation for the Cheltenham defeat a little over a month later when he was sent to Ayr for the Scottish Champion Hurdle where, despite the concession of 6 lb, he put the best part of five lengths between himself and Easby Abbey, who finished third behind Indianapolis, which was an improvement of nearly a stone on his Champion Hurdle run.

The following Monday, 16 April, the newspapers reported that 'Captain Christy, trained by Pat Taaffe and ridden by Bobby Beasley, made up for his third in the Champion Hurdle at Cheltenham by winning the Scottish Champion Hurdle at Ayr on Saturday in record time after a great battle with Indianapolis. He won by three parts of a length with favourite Easby Abbey – second at Cheltenham – a further four lengths away. He won in a time of 3 minutes 35.10 seconds.'

Bobby later said that the horse was as 'brave as a lion, in fact the bravest I've ever ridden, for the ground at Ayr was certainly not suitable for him'. Jane Samuel was quoted as saying, 'He will have one more outing over hurdles in France in June and then he will go chasing.'

Christy was sent to Auteil for the French Champion Hurdle that June, but he was fourth on very unsuitable firm going. After that he was put away for the rest of the summer prior to his chasing debut the following season.

Reminiscing from a vantage point nearly forty years later, Pat Murphy says he feels the good thing about the Champion Hurdle result was that it set Christy on the steeplechasing road.

'They felt that with the opposition the way it was at the time, he'd shown he was not going to beat them, so it was time to move on,' he says. 'If he had won that Champion Hurdle, Pat would have been under pressure to go back to Cheltenham again for another crack at it. And, even if he had won it, he would have been lucky to do so. In hindsight, therefore, it was the best thing for him not to have won it, because his career was then essentially mapped out for him.'

Analysing Christy's career to this point, Tom Taaffe is another to see patterns emerging – from the Pidcock era right through to Christy's new-found status as a potential legend.

'There was a pattern there where it became clear that the Major was no longer strong enough to ride him,' he says. 'The horse was running away with him on the gallops at home and doing the same on the racetrack. The Major had a few falls off the horse and he was just getting too old. When he couldn't ride him any more on the gallops or on the racetrack, he realised it was time to sell. The fun was gone out of it for him and if he couldn't ride him, he didn't want him.

'Christy's early career path was not exactly conventional, certainly by modern standards. He ran over all sorts of distances – on the flat and over hurdles. I don't know why that was. It might have had something to do with the Major or it might simply have been that they didn't realise exactly what they had on their hands. But, once they got proper jockeys up on him, a different pattern starts emerging and they got it right fairly quickly.

'The routine after the Sweeps win was predictable enough: Christy did not run again until the Scalp Hurdle and that was his only run before the Champion Hurdle.

'I was at national school in Kill the day he finished third in the Champion Hurdle and unfortunately there was no way of getting out of that and I didn't get to see the race – or even hear it on the radio – in the end. I had to run down to the bookie shop down the town – there were no phones available, especially not to us schoolboys – to try and find out how the horse had got on. I did not actually have any few bob on him that day. I remember at home that there was an expectation about Christy going to Cheltenham, especially after he won the Sweeps Hurdle.

'But they had travelled over knowing that Christy was on that upward curve you expect to see from a good horse. He had done everything right and it was felt he was a horse that could go the whole way. If you have a good one, it always shows through and looking back over the results prior to the Champion Hurdle, Christy had definitely shown a lot. I mean, he was unbeaten in four races going to Cheltenham, so they were not wrong to have high hopes. The other part to remember in all of this is that when the Major was riding Christy and the horse was running away with him and running wide and all that stuff, he never got a crack of a stick. The Major might have tried to hit him, but he couldn't hit him. Christy therefore never had a hard race for his first six or seven runs and they were really only educational experiments. Hence why he survived the distance at the other end,' Tom maintains.

He also agrees that as Christy had by now gone to the top of the handicap over hurdles, there was nothing more for him in that sphere. 'Either you focus solely on the Champion Hurdle or you move on,' he says. 'Once you leave the hurdling you're hoping the horse can jump a fence and if he can, then you could have anything.'

If Christy whiled away the hours in his paddock without a care on his young shoulders during that cool and damp summer, then Pat Taaffe, Pat Samuel and Bobby Beasley dreamed of what lay ahead, for each man knew they had a horse capable of fulfilling their diverse, but parallel, desires. For Pat Taaffe it was the dream of a horse capable of giving him as a trainer what Arkle had delivered to him as a jockey; for Pat Samuel it was the dream of having a horse everyone else in racing jealously craved; and, for Bobby Beasley, it was the dream of having a horse which would re-establish him as one of the legends of the track and allow him to put behind him the nightmare of the previous ten years of his life – for Bobby, this was big-time redemption.

Christy – Chasing Dreams

By now the level of interest that surrounded Captain Christy was, in some ways, unfortunate because the connections were absolutely plagued with constant press queries about the well-being of the horse. In another sense, however, it was all very predictable given the elements that combined to make the Captain Christy story irresistible for both the specialist media and the daily papers.

On the one hand you had a trainer who was universally loved not least for his riding of the much-mourned Arkle. While there was universal goodwill for him in his new career as a trainer, there were those who felt – with good reason – that he was too nice, too much of a gentleman, to prosper in such a harsh profession. Even so, he had been blessed at the very outset of his training career by having a superstar in his yard. If the mercurial Christy's natural flamboyance and talent sparked the imagination of the racing public, creating an appeal which had not been seen since Arkle's heyday, it was his unpredictable brilliance which bonded the horse to the broader public.

Throw in the Bobby factor – reformed drunk, with deep and dark personal problems, making a comeback at nearly forty years of age but once more showing he had the talent to compete at the very highest level – and you had a story which was captivating for both the public and the press and so every move by the trio was studiously observed.

The trouble was that Christy was so talented, the variety of options open to the connections was immense. While Bobby and Pat Taaffe wanted the horse to go chasing and stay at the game, there were still many lucrative hurdle races open to him, including a return to the Sweeps Hurdle at Leopardstown in December.

The public's desire to see their new hero return to the track was immense and they finally got their wish when Pat Taaffe announced that Christy would make his chasing bow on 1 November 1973 at Powerstown Park in Clonmel in the Magner, O'Brien and Moynihan Novice Chase against five other chasing rookies.

In the *Irish Press* that morning Tony Power told his readers, under a story headlined 'Captain Gets The Vote' that, while traditionally hurdle racers of championship class rarely make top class chasers, the signs were that Pat Taaffe's horse would make a smooth winning transition in this company.

'As the winner of the Irish Sweeps Hurdle and the Scottish Champion Hurdle and indeed his placing in the Champion Hurdle at Cheltenham, it makes one think immediately of the Dreaper star Flyingbolt which was placed at Cheltenham and went on to challenge the mighty Arkle in the chasing roll of honour.' It is an opinion that later would find credence.

This was high praise indeed, as Flyingbolt, also trained by Arkle's trainer Tom Dreaper, was once rated by the official handicapper as inferior to his stable companion by only 1 lb. Officially, Flyingbolt remains the second best National Hunt horse of all time (on official handicap ratings) and for Christy to be mentioned in comparison with him is an indication of just how good this unproven chaser could turn out to be.

Tony Power's assessment is underscored by none other than Ted Walsh, who maintains, 'Christy was not a good horse; he was a great horse. He was a phenomenal horse and I always tell people that after Arkle and Flyingbolt, the best horse I ever saw was Captain Christy.' High praise indeed, but while expectations of Christy were high, he still had a lot to do.

Christy had been given a schooling spin around Punchestown – with Bobby aboard – the week before his debut in Clonmel and it is fair to say that both jockey and trainer were confident going into his first chase. So too was the racing press and Christy was universally selected to win easily, with Phonsie O'Brien's Bernardsville seen as the only potential danger to the six-year-old.

A record crowd turned out at Powerstown Park to witness Christy's chasing debut, a credible sign of the manner in which the Irish public – racing and otherwise – had adopted Christy and the stories surrounding him. They were not disappointed as he trounced the field with an imperious display. At the end of the 2-mile-2-furlong contest Christy crossed the line while the second and third horses were only jumping the second last fence to win by a distance, prompting Bobby to exclaim, 'If I gave him a slap down the shoulder he'd have lapped them!'

The jockey did admit that Christy still had 'a lot to learn' about the jumping game as he had 'jumped very flat and treated the fences like hurdles'. He went on to say the race had been 'highly satisfactory' from his point of view and that he forgave Christy his only mistake – when hitting the last – 'as his concentration may have strayed with the huge crowd down there'.

Later on Bobby would reflect on the ride, saying 'in his first novice chase at Clonmel, he gave me a hair-raising ride. It was one of the most exciting races of my life, if you like that sort of thing! He took charge and, jumping like a wild thing and hurdling his fences at great speed, left the others miles behind. At one stage, he was three or four fences in front and, although he almost took the last out of the ground, he won as he liked.'

John Nicholson was at Powerstown Park that day and remembers the race vividly. 'He took the last out by the roots, but still won on the bridle. You'd have to say it was an impressive performance, but there were definite questions about his jumping, although he was such a strong horse he was able to hit a fence and not fall,' he says.

Pat Taaffe immediately pinpointed the Wills Premier Chase Qualifier at Punchestown the following Wednesday as Christy's next assignment before then sending the horse to Ascot for the Black and White Chase and then on to the Wills Premier Chase Final at Haydock the following January.

For all the delight and backslapping that followed the win, both trainer and jockey knew only too well that there was still a lot of work to be done with Christy to hone the talent he so obviously possessed.

Christy's victory aside, the Clonmel meeting was also notable for the fact that Pat Samuel's New Zealand-bred Yenesei made his hurdling debut in the opening race, the Cahir Hurdle. Tony Power in the *Irish Press* remarked that 'under top weight, this grey acquitted himself with distinction to finish third and when he becomes used to our type of hurdle, he will win good races'. He would also be instrumental in winning Pat Samuel a hell of a lot of money.

The main focus was on Christy, however, and his next race came just a week after his seasonal return. And the day before that second race the newspapers gave quite a deal of space to the fact that Fred Winter's Bula had made a very successful chasing debut at Lingfield, winning by twenty lengths and delighting his trainer and jockey Richard Pitman.

The victory was also noted in the previews for the Wills Premier Chase (Qualifier) at Punchestown on 7 November where, while Christy was universally selected by the various racing correspondents as the likely winner, it was mentioned that after Bula's 'splendid' trial for the Black and White Gold Cup at Ascot, the onus would now be on the Irish horse to confirm his growing reputation.

Tony Power in the *Irish Press* noted that Christy was also bound for the valuable Ascot contest but that he would be taking on opposition which was considerably stiffer than in his first chase. He highlighted Our Greenwood, Hey Bob and Boom Docker as the biggest threats.

Michael O'Farrell made more of the possible clash between the former hurdle rivals at Ascot but, in fairness, was more interested in what Christy was going to do on his second chasing outing and wondered if he would repeat 'his rather staggering tearaway Clonmel antics'. He suggested that, as the Punchestown fences were rather more difficult than those in the Tipperary venue, 'a mistake or two would add a little caution to his undoubted attributes of strength and bravery'.

A twenty-length win over Boom Docker and Lupus Vulpus might sound like a comprehensive performance, but this was not a straightforward race as Christy's learning curve continued on a steep, upward trajectory.

To close observers the win in Clonmel was a case of the headstrong beast doing as he liked, dictating the take-off and landing points to the jockey. This time around it was Bobby doing the dictating. Christy was interfered with at the third fence and unnerved slightly when Even Choice, contesting the lead with him, blundered and impeded him. Then, going to the fence opposite the stands Our Greenwood unintentionally squeezed Christy, but 'the burly six-year-old' had the talent and intelligence to get clear of trouble. Both incidents showed how much Christy had learned in a very short period of time and he had the large Punchestown crowd buzzing with an exemplary display of jumping – apart, typically, from fiddling the third last – and when Our Greenwood fell, he was left with a clear lead and won easily.

'I was able to pick him up and ride him today,' Bobby said after the horse had been given what *The Irish Times* described as 'an Arkle-like reception' in the winners' enclosure. 'This was a great improvement and we have hit it off to perfection. He must take a deal of beating in any company.'

Pat Taaffe's reaction to the victory and the possibility of taking on Bula at Ascot was very much of the 'bring it on' variety, albeit in the trainer's characteristic understated way. 'We beat Bula twice over hurdles so why should we not beat him over fences?' he commented succinctly.

The Punchestown meeting was also notable for the fact that a horse who would much later feature greatly in Christy's career, Jim Dreaper's Ten Up, made what was described as 'a splendid chasing debut' in the Neills' Gorse Chase.

And, a few days later, on 15 November, *The Irish Times* reporting from the Ballsbridge Goffs' Sales, said that a full brother of Christy's – an unnamed chestnut colt by Mon Capitaine and Christy's Bow – was bought by Roy McNeill from Newry, County Down, for 9,000 guineas. The horse was the top lot of the day. The paper described the purchase as being an own-brother to the new Arkle, Captain Christy. Interestingly, Roy McNeill was one of those who had expressed an interest in buying Christy himself prior to his sale to Pat Samuel.

Like much of Mon Capitaine's other progeny that horse

never proved to be any good, but Christy's winning ways were certainly good news for breeder George Williams who was finally making a bit of profit from the sire of 'the new Arkle'.

That said, Christy himself was the subject of much interest in the run-up to the race at Ascot on Saturday 17 November as the press was getting very excited about the clash between himself and Bula, which was now being flagged as the biggest Anglo-Irish racing confrontation since the days of Arkle and Mill House and a race which had thoroughly captured the imagination of the racing public.

The 2-mile Black and White Chase was a very prestigious affair anyway – it had been won the previous year by Pendil, ridden by Richard Pitman, who would ride Bula this time around in place of Paul Kelleway – and the difference of opinions among the Irish and English racing writers about the potential outcome could not have been wider.

The English recognised Christy as a special but wayward talent and reckoned Bula to be the more refined jumper. They were certainly not incorrect in this assertion, but the main reason they fancied their horse was because under the rules of the race, he would be handicapped 10 lb lighter than his Irish rival – a penalty Christy received for having won his two races over fences.

For their part, the Irish maintained that what was said to be the 'majestic authority' with which Christy had won his two novice chases would prove to be the difference between the two rivals, although it has to be said that there was widespread concern in the Irish media about how the 10 lb weight differential could affect their hero.

Even so, Tony Power in the *Irish Press* concluded his preview by stating baldly that Christy would 'gallop the others into the ground by his pace-forcing tactics' and that his would be the decisive factor as the Irish hope was a front-runner and Bula had to be held up for a late run.

Unlike his last outing to England, Christy travelled reasonably well and did not fret unduly. But he did sweat up badly before the start of the race and Bobby reported that he got himself into 'a terrible state'.

Then a terrible blunder by Christy at the second last fence in the race unseated Bobby and handed Bula an easy twenty-length victory. There was little consolation for the connections afterwards: they all felt they would have won if their horse had stood up. Bobby in particular was inconsolable because he felt he had been responsible for the mistake. 'I asked him to stand off too far,' he mulled. Pat Samuel tried to take the sting out it for Bobby by responding, 'You couldn't dictate to Christy and no one could have survived the error he made.'

If the Irish were disconsolate, Bula's connections were cock-a-hoop and Richard Pitman maintained afterwards that 'Bula was running away when it happened. I was just sitting there. I only wish Captain Christy had stood up. Bula was simply fantastic.'

Trainer Fred Winter echoed these sentiments, saying 'the horse jumped brilliantly and he made ground at every fence'. However, he dismissed the possibility of Bula being tried over longer distances and insisted his Cheltenham target would be the Arkle Challenge Trophy over 2 miles.

For those Christy fans back in Ireland, the race was a big disappointment and while those close to the horse knew his foibles only too well, for others – watching on television – it was the first time they had witnessed the brilliance of his jumping on the one hand and his complete disregard for the big fences on the other.

'Going chasing with Christy was not without its moments –

either schooling or racing, let me tell you, and he proved it that day,' says Pat Murphy. 'He'd won his chasing debut at Clonmel and then he won at Punchestown, which was a very good performance. Then, of course, he went to Ascot for the Black and White and that was the first time that the public had seen what Christy was capable of *not* doing at a fence; he didn't have a whole heap of respect for anything in his life and every now and then he showed he'd no respect for a fence either. I remember being in the Dew Drop Inn in Kill watching it on television and a huge groan went up when he hit the second last – walked straight through it. Of course, Christy found a leg and stood up, not a bother on him, but he lost Bobby – big time.'

Bobby continued to blame himself for the fall. 'He was not going as well as Bula when we came to the second last. So I thought I must jump that one well to have any chance and, forgetting that he was a novice, I was sitting too far up his neck and I asked him to stand too far off. He put down and I went on without him. I'd paid the penalty for over-confidence.'

Looking back on it now, Pat Samuel reckons that Bobby was being very harsh in blaming himself for the error. 'Whatever about being asked for a big jump at that second last, nobody could have stayed on him, especially when you think about the way he had gone down.'

Interestingly on the same day that Christy fell at Ascot, his former owners, the Nicholsons, had a very big winner at Leopardstown when their Bigaroon won the November Handicap, but there was now going to be a change of tack for their one-time pride and joy as Christy was about to revert to flights in an attempt to regain his Irish Sweeps Hurdle title.

His preparation for that came on 8 December when he was entered for the Benson and Hedges Hurdle at Fairyhouse where the conditions on the day were desperately wet and the official going was soft. On top of that, Christy was allotted 12 stone 7 lb and, against old foes such as Maddenstown and Brendon's Road, that was widely viewed as being too big an ask for the horse.

It was but Christy went down heroically by just four lengths to Maddenstown, to whom he was giving nearly 3 stone in weight. He led from the off and ran gallantly at the front until the final fence when Tommy Burns' charge hunted him down and took the lead on the run-in. The Irish papers were impressed by what they had seen, especially given the conditions of the ground and the added weight Christy was asked to carry. Pat Taaffe, too, was pleased, 'I am completely satisfied with the performance. It was a grand effort and now, after the Sweeps Hurdle, I will probably go for the Wills Premier Chase at Haydock before Cheltenham.'

What the trainer omitted to mention was which race he was considering for Christy at the festival meeting. As the horse was only a novice, it was expected that the 2-mile Arkle Chase would be the obvious target, but the race at Fairyhouse had put in his mind a far more taxing challenge.

All that was blown to the four winds the following day, however, when the Taaffe family was engulfed with appalling tragedy. On 9 December Pat and Molly's third daughter, Joanna, was taken to St Vincent's Hospital in Dublin, having suddenly and mysteriously lapsed into a coma at home in Alasty. She died within hours at the age of just thirteen.

Understandably, Olive and Tom, respectively Joanna's older sister and younger brother, have particularly vivid memories of the time and of the devastating effect the calamity had on their parents and the household as a whole – not only at the time, but into the future as well.

'Joanna died in the middle of the whole Captain Christy story and I'd say that had a big influence on everything. We were in boarding school at the time – Mount Sackville in

Chapelizod – and it was Joanna's first year there. A couple of weeks previously she had hit her head off a table-tennis table at school – it did not seem a big deal – but because of the nature of the business my father was in, my mother would always have been conscious of head injuries. So she brought Joanna to hospital to have it X-rayed, but they didn't find anything wrong.

'Then we were at home for a long weekend and Joanna spent most of the time just lounging on the couch. Nobody thought much of it, but then she went into a coma, was taken to hospital and she never came home,' she remembers sadly.

Tom would have been closer to Joanna in age and he too remembers the tragic events. 'Joanna died just before Christmas in 1973. She was complaining of headaches and was given a few aspirin before she went to bed and she never woke up the following morning. It was about half nine or ten o'clock the following morning when we realised there was something wrong and that she had gone into a coma. Unfortunately she never came out of it.'

The Ireland of that time was a very different place from that which exists today and attitudes were far less enlightened than is now the case. A catastrophic event of this nature was borne with resignation and stoicism within the Taaffe family. Emotions were never allowed their full voice and consequently got unhealthily bottled up. Pat and Molly Taaffe were no different from others of their generation in this regard and whatever issues there may have been with regard to their child's untimely death were never discussed.

'In those days nobody really talked about anything like that,' Olive says. 'I don't think my mother ever visited her grave afterwards – I don't think she could bring herself to do so – and it was never discussed at home. Things are very different today, obviously, and it is more healthy now. But that's the way it was. Her death was never explained to us and we were never told what had happened. I think there was some apology issued down the line from the medical people, but I do not know the details. Today if something like that happened, there would be some sort of investigation; but in those days the doctors were always right in anything they did or said and they were never questioned.'

Tom points to the obvious but unspoken desolation wreaked on his parents – both at the time and going forward and how the effects of Joanna's death affected them terribly.

'There were all sorts going on around then. My parents, God love them, they just crashed. There was a big "blame" thing going on with them – no more than there would be now in more "enlightened times" – especially as they felt they should have spotted that something was wrong at an earlier stage. But that's the way life is. I remember being up and around that very morning and I recall going up to the bedroom to tell her we were having tea, or something, and she was still asleep. A while later they went up to see why she was still asleep and realised something was amiss. I never realised she was in a coma when I saw her that morning and that was the last time I saw her. She was taken away in an ambulance. She was alive for a day or so in the hospital and I was not allowed near the place. It just tore my parents apart and it was after that that my mother went downhill. It put a big hole in my father. Obviously what would happen over the next couple of months would be great for everyone involved, but that was terribly ironic given what had happened.'

The death notice in *The Irish Times* of Monday 10 December 1973 read 'TAAFFE (Alasty House, Straffan, Co. Kildare) December 9, 1973 at St Vincent's Hospital, Elm Park, Dublin, Joanna, aged 13 years, beloved daughter of Molly and Pat;

deeply regretted by her loving parents, brothers, sisters, uncles, aunts, cousins and a large circle of friends. RIP. Remains were removed yesterday (Sunday) to St Brigid's Church, Kill. Funeral after 3 oc Mass today to St Corban's Cemetery, Naas. House and funeral private. No letters please.'

The time is also well remembered by Pat Murphy, then a lad in the yard at Alasty. His recall is tempered by the emotion of a similar tragedy which occurred to his own daughter Melissa – she was knocked down by a car, having disembarked from a school bus in February 2001, just months before he recorded his biggest training success when Supreme Glory won the Welsh Grand National.

'Unfortunately, I have had the same experience myself as they had,' he says. 'I lost a daughter in a car accident when she was just fourteen. I can now relate to exactly how the Taaffes felt. It was awkward for us in the yard to be seen to be enjoying anything much with such a dark cloud hanging over the place. And I know now from personal experience that no matter what sort of person you are, it is not something you're ever going to stop thinking about. And Mrs Taaffe was a lovely, lovely woman, but it had a bad effect on her. It is a terrible thing that you have to experience it yourself to know what it does to people. I've been lucky enough to come out the far side of it, but it is not something that everybody can deal with and the Taaffes did not deal with it very well. Obviously it would have been a huge shock and they dealt with it the only way they knew how at the time.'

Pat Taaffe dealt with it by throwing himself back into his work and by keeping his horses on the boil.

'The whole thing came at what should have been a fantastic time for the Taaffes, but I think the one bit of sanity throughout it all was an insane horse. Christy was the driving force to get

Pat Taaffe out every single day and to have a purpose in life. It was a horrible time for them and, as my own experience has taught me, it is not something everyone can come through,' Pat Murphy says.

In the weeks that followed, as the National Hunt season ramped up, the issues dictating the races each horse would run in at Cheltenham became clearer. On 22 December Bula won the Benson and Hedges Novices' Chase – another four-horse affair – and the following Monday the speculation across the papers was that he might now be sent to Cheltenham for the Gold Cup. Fred Winter said after Sandown that Bula would be nominated for the race and he would be talking to the owner about it. 'Personally, I don't want him to run in it and I think it might be asking too much of a novice,' he said, adding that the horse would also be entered for the Arkle and the Sun Alliance Champion Novices' Chase. Undoubtedly this gem of news coming from England further encouraged Pat Taaffe, Pat Samuel and Bobby to think again about what Cheltenham contest they would enter Christy in.

Pat Samuel maintains that after the disaster at Ascot the idea of the Gold Cup had not entered their minds but as the season progressed, all that changed.

They reasoned amongst themselves that they felt Christy would have beaten Bula at Ascot if he had not unseated Bobby and they also felt cocky about their chances against Pendil and The Dikler. So the collective thinking was 'why not enter him for the Gold Cup?' They discussed it anxiously amongst themselves and, although they did not admit it publicly, they certainly thought it was a decision they could justify if they had to.

For the moment though, they remained focussed on the Sweeps Hurdle at Leopardstown on 27 December where

Christy would, once again, face rivals such as Champion Hurdle winner Comedy Of Errors, Brendon's Road and Ryan Price's Moonlight Bay, another English challenger. Interestingly, Yenesei, Pat Samuel's New Zealand-bred grey was also entered and several observers felt this would take some of the 'collar work' off Christy in what were expected to be testing conditions.

Pat Murphy reckons that the return to hurdles was something Pat Taaffe was not altogether comfortable with, but he went along with the owners' wishes.

'Ascot was the first time the television public had seen him, but Pat [Samuel] felt that the horse had lost a big opportunity and he decided to send him back over hurdles as he attempted to regain his Sweeps Hurdle crown. Again I was not privy to the decision, but certainly everyone in the yard felt Pat was under pressure from the Samuels to go back over hurdles at that time. I remember that there was a lot of gossip about Comedy Of Errors, that he might not be ready for the race and I'm sure this impinged on their thinking – especially if they thought there was a soft race to be won.

'I know that Bobby, from talking to him later in life, never thought it was the wisest thing in the world to do – taking a horse beginning his chasing career back over hurdles. He didn't think that was the ideal thing to do. In the heel of the hunt, his third place there under top weight was a massive performance and when you consider the ground wasn't his preferred best and that there were really good horses in the race, it was actually the best piece of form going into the Gold Cup. In terms of the sheer ability, that told you where the horse stood in the pecking order.'

Tom Taaffe too – even now – wonders about the wisdom of the decision. 'Sure, he was a novice and he was being trained as such. Of course, they did think he was still good enough that season to win the Sweeps Hurdle again and that it would fit in to the programme. The thing is that with a horse who is a dodgy jumper it was not the best road to go because it gives him bad habits again and you're letting him out of jail. Then you've got to go back over fences and the horse starts hurdling them again. It would not have been the road I went down.'

The public did not know at the time, but Pat Taaffe had been fretting slightly about Christy in the week coming up to the race. Bobby would later maintain the trainer had told him Christy was running a temperature, but it seems very unlikely. It may have been that there were concerns about the horse not being 100 per cent, but there is nothing to suggest that Pat Taaffe would have knowingly run the horse if he thought it was under par, even if he was under pressure from the owners.

In any event Christy ran a relatively listless race to finish third behind the two horses he had beaten the previous year and while there was some media speculation to the effect that the horse 'was not at his best', the trainer himself would only say that 'of course, I am a bit disappointed, but he will have another day and will now go back over fences for the Wills Premier Chase Final'.

Bobby later insisted that the horse had coughed after the Ascot race and 'was never firing' at Leopardstown. 'Half a mile from home he was out on his feet and it was only dogged determination that carried him into third place,' he said.

Interestingly, Yenesei (whose name most journalists found impossible to spell correctly) finished fourth behind Christy and just two days later went on to beat future Grand National winner L'Escargot in the Morgiana Hurdle at Punchestown off a top weight of 12 stone in a race in which Bobby was reported to have given him 'a magnificently strong ride'.

And so the New Year came and went and talk of the

forthcoming Cheltenham Festival in the media centred on the fact that there appeared to be no obvious Irish 'banker' ahead of the great festival. Indeed, Michael O'Farrell in *The Irish Times* went so far as to say that the Irish could 'immediately say goodbye to the Champion Hurdle and the Gold Cup for the Hurdle rests between Lanzarote and Comedy Of Errors, while Pendil only has to stand up to win the Cup, or so it would appear'.

He further speculated that, in the remaining races, Christy immediately sprang to mind, but he wondered would he clash once more with Bula who, 'at Ascot, certainly looked to have his measure when the Irish horse threw away any chance he had at the second last fence'.

Such was the situation just two months before the festival that thoughts of Christy running there in anything other than one of the novice chases, was deemed absurd unless, of course, like Pat Taaffe, Pat Samuel and Bobby, you were already thinking well outside the box.

There were, of course, plenty of people willing to tell them why they should not go for the Gold Cup and the reasons why they should not have are lucidly voiced by Willie Robinson: 'Christy hurdled his fences and he never got back on his hocks and jumped them. At the time nobody ran novices in big races, apart maybe from Fred Rimell. Christy really bent his fences and I can promise you the fences in Cheltenham were very solid obstacles; they were not ordinary bush fences like they had here where you could gallop through them.' His was a view supported by many others – apart from Christy's connections.

Pat Samuel maintains strenuously that as each day passed he was erring on the side of sending the horse to the Gold Cup, even if his trainer was thinking more along the lines of a tilt at it the following year as, in 1974, he would be quite satisfied if

Christy won the Arkle or the Sun Alliance.

'My thinking was that the horse was beating the other novices – when he stood up – by a furlong, so let's have a go,' Samuel recalls. The debate, however, was far from being over.

The events of 19 January 1974 would only serve to give ammunition to those naysayers who felt that Christy was a great but flawed horse and that his sometimes alarming jumping traits would prevent him from ever winning anything worthwhile again. The evidence to support such an argument came at Haydock that Saturday when Christy was the hot favourite to win the Wills Premier Chase and follow in the footsteps of previous Irish winners such as L'Escargot, Colebridge and Leap Frog.

Back then Haydock was a fearsome track and Tom Taaffe is still awestruck that it was decided to send Christy to the Lancashire venue. 'Haydock, in those days, was the stiffest track in England. Up until they changed the fences a few years ago, they had difficulty in getting chasers to go there because most of them couldn't get around the place. Novice chasers wouldn't go there and there used to be all sorts of incentives for trainers to get them to run their chasers there. But back in their day …'

Previews pointed out that even though the 2½ mile trip over Haydock's notoriously stiff 'drop fences' (these were two very robust obstacles, which had a much lower landing area than the take-off point) was short of Christy's best, he should win handily and thus he was sent off the 8/11 favourite. He jumped off boldly into the lead and was fencing with characteristic aplomb when Bobby allowed him to stretch for home fully a mile out. But, at the second last he got too close to the fence and then slipped on landing on the far side of it. Bobby was pitched out of the saddle and onto the turf. 'He would have walked it,' the dejected jockey reported later.

'The ground was too firm for him and I let him go on,' Bobby explained. 'I wished afterwards that I'd held him up, but he was standing off and really pinging his fences. Coming to the second last he was a certainty, but he was tiring and I said to him, "It was my fault at Ascot. This time I won't ask you for a long one." He put in a short one, hit the top of the fence and, deceived by the drop, came down.'

As it was, Christy continued without his jockey and actually crossed the line first, giving a lead to the eventual winner, Credibility, ridden by none other than Richard Pitman, who commented, 'I was fifteen lengths behind Captain Christy and when I got over the fence Bobby Beasley was already on his feet with his hands on his hips, shaking his head in disbelief. I didn't want Credibility to be out on his own so soon, but fortunately the riderless Captain Christy came along to give me the lead I needed. When he fell I had no chance of catching him.'

Pat Taaffe was philosophical. 'That's racing,' he commented succinctly. 'He'll go to Punchestown next month and then could possibly go for the Leopardstown Chase before a tilt at Cheltenham.' Despite this latest failure, his faith in the horse remained undimmed, but his frustration was manifest.

Pat Murphy remembers there was desolation among the staff in the yard after the race, but reckons it was tempered with some realism. 'Let's face it, Haydock at that time was not a place to be taking a chance with a fence – and he did take a chance with one or two, to be fair to him. You could always – as a jockey – blame yourself for an awful lot of the things he'd done. But Christy was the type of horse who could fool you into thinking you'd made the mistake,' he says.

Bobby later recalled that, on the way back to Manchester Airport with Pat Taaffe in the taxi, he realised how much store he had set on the Cheltenham Gold Cup and was very depressed.

'It was my fault that we hadn't won at Ascot and Haydock. I'd let my horse down as well as my old friend Pat. This was the first real test of AA's teaching because normally after that sort of day I'd have drowned my sorrows. It never even entered my head. As I got into the taxi beside him, I said to Pat, "Jesus, that was a desperate day." He too was sunk in gloom. I shook myself mentally. No depression. There's no point in going on the booze for something that's gone. That's a negative attitude. You want a positive approach. Go forward. Attack.'

Many years later, Bobby would tell writer Ivor Herbert that the spectre of the Ascot and Haydock races still kept him awake at night. 'That race still haunts me. The Ascot thing came back [at Haydock] – I let him fiddle. It's the oldest mistake in the world. When in doubt – ask! If I'd been in my prime Christy would have won both those races,' he recalled dolefully.

If Christy's performance at Haydock that day had been disappointing, the same was true of Yenesei's. A heavily backed 85/40 favourite, he ran in the Cigar Handicap Hurdle the same day and was soundly beaten. The horse was held up in the early stages and when Bobby asked him for an effort three hurdles out, he was a spent force and finished seventh of the eight runners.

The journey home from the Liverpool track was a very long one for Pat Taaffe and Bobby as they contemplated the state of play with regards to their Cheltenham hopes. Prior to the day's racing there were many options open to them for both Christy and Yenesei; afterwards, it appeared, many of those options had vanished. But, as Bobby said, the only way forward was with a positive approach.

In his 'English Notebook' column in the *Irish Field* the following week, Jonathan Powell wrote that until his unexpected departure Christy had jumped with a mixture of boldness and economy that had all his rivals deep in trouble before the final turn. 'Surely, if there is any justice, he must win a top-class novice chase in Britain before the season is over.'

'It is always a disappointment when you fall in a race that you look like winning,' Pat Samuel would later reflect. 'But I've had plenty of that over the years and I got used to the idea of that sort of thing happening. I don't remember being particularly upset at the time, especially as he had actually performed so well before being caught out by those Haydock fences.'

For the moment though, it was back to novice chasing for Christy and Bobby and next up was the Poulaphouca Novice Chase at Punchestown on 8 February. The racing press was unanimous in its feeling that both horse and jockey needed a confidence-boosting performance to get back on track. The accepted feeling then was that Christy would be aimed at the Sun Alliance Novice Chase at Cheltenham and Michael O'Farrell said in *The Irish Times* that if he was to be successful there, then he needed to be foot-perfect at Punchestown.

Tony Power in the *Irish Press* was of a similar mind and said, in a tone fully compliant with the republican nature of the paper, that the two falls in Britain 'had to be atoned for'. Even so, he predicted Christy would win and beat Perpol, who had recently beaten Ten Up at Leopardstown.

Well, win he did, but he left his supporters and his connections with very mixed feelings in doing so. His jumping was very inconsistent throughout and at the early fences in the 2-mile-4-furlong event, he dived left at some, giving Bobby a very hairy time of it. But Bobby used his patience and guile to settle the horse, whereupon he produced some fantastic jumps before reverting to form at the final ditch where he met the fence all wrong but was clever enough to put in a short stride before popping the obstacle.

Power commented in the *Irish Press* the following Monday

that Christy had too much courage. 'He has a gay, reckless abandon and now Taaffe will send him to Thurles for the PZ Mower Chase before going to Cheltenham for the Sun Alliance Chase.'

Similarly, Michael O'Farrell was unimpressed by Christy's jumping that day, but enthused by the victory.

'Taking the first fence low, screwing to the left at the fourth, another violent swerve at the next, meeting the last ditch wrong and hurdling several others would appear to be a damning indictment of Captain Christy's jumping prowess, yet the extraordinary horse spread-eagled the field to win the Poulaphouca Chase by twenty lengths,' he wrote in *The Irish Times*.

'He is a very difficult horse to ride,' he quoted Bobby Beasley as saying. 'A very erratic horse – just no pattern to his jumping and he hurdles his fences. He's going to take time.'

He too pinpointed the Sun Alliance as Christy's most likely Cheltenham target and at that point it is fair to say that was what was in Pat Taaffe's mind also. But the previous Friday, the initial entry list for the Gold Cup had been published with seventeen runners pencilled in, including Christy. All options were being kept open, as the entry for the Sun Alliance had also been made.

But then the waters became muddier as the news broke on 11 February that Bula had sustained an injury when falling in the Stone's Ginger Wine Handicap Chase at Sandown. He lost his unbeaten record over fences and was now doubtful for Cheltenham. Fred Winter issued the news to the Press Association and it made headlines.

If Bula did not make Cheltenham, surely the Sun Alliance was there for the taking for Christy? Perhaps not, because the papers reported on 14 February that Ladbrokes had trimmed his Gold Cup odds from 33/1 to 20/1 after laying Christy to lose £30,000 after 'heavy backing in London'.

Having jumped so badly at Punchestown, it was obvious that Christy needed more schooling and Pat Taaffe and Bobby put him through a series of intensive schools at home at Alasty before sending him to Leopardstown for an on-course school after racing there on 23 February. It was not impressive.

Pat Murphy laughs at the memory of that schooling session. 'Pat had organised a school at Leopardstown and this was to be his last serious piece of work before Cheltenham. The horse jumped three fences and then dropped his shoulder, dumped Bobby, and walked back up the path to the paddock minus the jockey. He wasn't having a bit of it. And that was supposed to be his last bit of serious schooling gallop before Cheltenham! But without Bobby and Pat, the horse would have done a lot more of that, but they understood him, they knew how to get the best out of him and how to look after him. The key to Christy was keeping him happy – mentally and physically – all the time.'

The *Irish Press* even carried a story about that schooling session – a reflection of the public interest in Christy's career, which was most unusual at the time. Under the headline 'Christy Fails To Please' the report outlined how Christy had initially jumped eight fences on his own before being joined by Champion Chase hopeful Leap Frog to jump six more.

'Lack of competition may have affected Captain Christy, but until joining Leap Frog he gave a lacklustre performance and blotted his copybook when unseating Bobby Beasley at the sixth fence on his solo run. Prior to that he had dived left at a number of fences, but this time ducked the other way, obviously having his eye on the gate back into the paddock. Leap Frog jumped when working with Captain Christy and his presence brought the Captain on a great deal.'

The following Thursday Christy travelled to Thurles for the PZ Mower Chase amid growing speculation that the Samuels were intent on ignoring Pat Taaffe's advice and committing their horse to the Gold Cup rather than any of the novice options. Although there had been little speculation in the press about such an eventuality, there had been constant whispers in the parade rings up and down the country that the 'mad' couple were willing to have a crack at Cheltenham's biggest prize.

Those rumours – for once – were not far wide of the mark, as Pat Samuel himself confirms. 'I used to ask Pat Taaffe where to put him, but he did not want to run him in the Gold Cup because he reckoned he was a certainty to win the Arkle. I said, "Listen, he's beating his own class by a furlong in every race he's in, so stick him in the Gold Cup now. He might be dead next year." So he did.'

On the morning of the Thurles race the papers were unanimous in their support for him. Tony Power in the *Irish Press* reckoned that 'it would be tempting fate to oppose' the horse and says that 'surely his participation in the Gold Cup depends on this performance'.

The Irish Times, describing Christy as the 'most talked about Irish steeplechaser since Arkle', said that the horse 'must win today with some authority to have any business crossing the channel for a tilt at Pendil and company'.

Both papers went into detail about Christy's questionable jumping record – particularly the embarrassing unseating at the recent Leopardstown schooling session – and *The Irish Times* even said the horse did 'not appear to be learning much from his experience'. Tony Power even went so far as to select Jim Dreaper's Good Review as the likely winner. Dreaper had three horses in the race – Good Review, Thyestes Chase winner Vulforo and Poker Game – and Power maintained that as Good Review was among the best jumpers in the country and Christy's jumping record was still suspect, he was taking a chance in nominating Good Review to win.

What the papers did not know was that Pat Taaffe and Bobby Beasley had been working hard at home to try and cure Christy's waywardness. They were trying all sorts of headgear, collars and bits that would not only give Bobby the control necessary to keep Christy jumping straight and true, but would also give the horse added confidence in the rider.

Pat remembered a horse from his past that had a habit of diving across his fences, but was cured of the trait by the adoption of a four-ring bit (Pat Samuel remembers it as a double ring snaffle bit), so he decided to give it a try at a rain-sodden Thurles. Whatever it was, it worked.

In the race Christy led to the first fence before Even Choice took up the running with Christy tracking him a few lengths back. There was pandemonium at the first ditch with three runners hitting the deck, including Dreaper pair Vulforo and Poker Game, along with Lanarhone Prince.

Bobby made his move as the remaining runners approached the fourth last fence and quickly made ground into the lead with Good Review giving chase. Entering the straight, Christy eased away from the field before giving everyone present a major heart attack when he put in a short stride at the last fence, barely took off and then crashed through the obstacle. Bobby was alive to the situation, however, and picked Christy off the ground and rode him home to a ten-length win.

Tony Power reported in the *Irish Press* of 1 March that Christy jumped 'straight and true' to win the PZ Mower Chase. This was obviously not the case, but it was evident the change of tack had had a profound effect.

'A change of equipment,' Power said, 'was a major factor in

improving his style and he ran without the overneck which was becoming his trademark and instead sported a four-ring bit.'

The net effect of the win was that the trainer announced in the winners' enclosure that Christy was now 'a certain Gold Cup Challenger'.

'I would not mind his mistake at the last,' Pat Taaffe said, 'and the Cheltenham fences have a take-off bar and that will make him stand off. He will have every encouragement to jump even better.'

Indeed, both jockey and trainer were very happy with the Thurles outcome and Bobby was tempted to compare Christy with Roddy Owen, the horse he rode to victory in the 1959 Gold Cup. 'He always reminded me of Roddy Owen,' he said, '[he's] very similar in mentality, if not physically. He had me on the floor four times in schooling before he won the Leopardstown Chase and then the Gold Cup.'

He also predicted that Christy would 'perform better over the bigger fences at Cheltenham' and with more pace in the race. 'He was grand today, I could do anything with him,' Bobby said. He also revealed that there had been a reason for the last-minute blunder as Christy's back legs had slipped when he went to stand off the fence and the horse was forced to put in a short stride just to get launched.

Secretly Bobby felt he 'was the only person in the world who knew that if everything went right, Christy would beat them all' at Cheltenham.

One interested observer at Thurles was Dr Austin Darragh, the man largely responsible for getting Bobby fit to ride again. Worried by all these last-fence blunders, Darragh (who was a fine horseman in his own right and whose late son, Paul was an international showjumper before his untimely death) recommended that Bobby change his stance on the horse to allow him cope with potential last-fence blunders. It was invaluable advice.

Pat Samuel remembers with considerable pride that the decision to send Christy to the Cheltenham Festival for its biggest prize caused a 'national sensation'. He rather liked that sort of thing. However, the decision also provoked considerable media analysis and in *The Irish Times* the following day, Michael O'Farrell was prompted to say of the Thurles performance that it certainly displayed more potential than previous outings. 'Granted, then, a clear round in the Gold Cup, it would not surprise me to see this good class jumper go close to winning. Certainly he was a different horse [at Thurles] to that headstrong character we have been seeing,' he opined.

Perhaps the most telling post-race breakdown of the race came in the *Irish Field* the following Saturday when Dave Baker said, 'The favourite had settled very well and for once seemed of like mind with his rider. There were none of the usual "dives" at fences and he rarely left a true line even when in the air. Captain Christy jumped in approved style and just when I decided he learned what chasing was all about, he reverted to character at the last. I would not rush in to back him for Cheltenham, where a mistake like the one at the last would in all probability see him grounded.'

A further comment on the decision to go for the Gold Cup came in the *Sunday Press* that week, when Tony O'Hehir described it as being 'a bold move'. He maintained that while the Samuels obviously loved a challenge, it was still difficult to reconcile the change in Cheltenham plans in view of the horse's chasing record to date.

'As his three victories over fences indicate, "the Captain" has ability to burn,' O'Hehir said. 'His jumping, however, has been most inconsistent resulting in falls on his two visits to

England and resulting in severe palpitations for his connections and supporters.

'Captain Christy is a horse that leaves one with conflicting opinions. The impressive way he can gallop opposition into the ground (his three wins over fences were achieved by a total of around eighty lengths) creates visions of potential greatness, but the erratic jumping dampens the enthusiasm considerably.

'The only reason I cannot see Captain Christy winning the Gold Cup this year is his jumping and in a three-and-a-quarter-miles race run at a fast gallop against animals such as Pendil, The Dikler and Inkslinger, there will be no room for chancy jumping.'

To this day O'Hehir reckons taking on the Gold Cup was a risky proposition for Christy's connections. 'It was a big deal that he was a novice in the race and a lot of people dismissed him because of that,' he says.

Pat Murphy reflects that even from within the yard, the waters were never anything less than muddy as all the options were weighed up.

'None of it was plain sailing – actually getting to the Gold Cup, from what I can remember. There was plenty of pressure being put on from all sides. Here was a horse which was far from straightforward with a jockey who'd been at the brink or over it and a trainer who was associated with the great Arkle. It was just that fairy tale waiting to happen, but there was huge pressure with it.

'It was a brave step at the time even just to enter him in the Gold Cup, because, let's face it, his only attempt at a three mile chase had been a total disaster. So to step him up to three and a quarter miles, when the furthest distance he had won over was two and a half, was again a massive leap in faith. But, they really believed in him. I was too young to appreciate or to know whether the horse was capable of doing what was being asked of him, but what I do know is that Pat and Bobby had more confidence going into the Gold Cup than they had going to the Champion Hurdle the previous year. There was actually a genuine sense of expectation throughout the yard going into the Gold Cup, plus – and it is no different now than it was then – as the race got closer there were press men coming down to us, TV crews and so on. The thing was that there was a huge buzz every time the horse left the yard. Pat, great master of understatement that he was, was very cool and calm about it – on the outside at least. Richard Cullen was the same. He was the head lad at the time and he used to take the horse to the races. He was the sort of fella who would never say two words if one would do, but he never got overexcited about anything.'

Looking at the whole situation from his current position as one of Ireland's top trainers, Tom Taaffe says he doesn't know what the take was on the decision to go for the Gold Cup.

'It was a huge thing to go from winning novice chases to winning things like the PZ Mower Chase. Back then the PZ was a much bigger race than it is now and it was a serious race – a Grade 1 – in those days. The thinking of most trainers would be that if by some chance the horse was beaten by Grade A novice horses, then they would have a good chance of getting their animal well handicapped but my father did not think that way. The thing was that throughout that period the horse was truly blooming; he was getting bigger and stronger in front of our eyes. He had also improved in all his work and they knew this thing was a machine. They knew it was tricky to keep it balanced, but it was still a machine nonetheless.'

Looking out his kitchen window at Portree Stables at the land where he now trains and where his father used the same hill – just on the other side of the hedge – to hone Christy. 'I was lucky enough to acquire this farm at Portree – on my father's advice – and to think that two different champions worked up different sides of the hill is amazing. Christy used to tank up that hill out there.'Bobby and Pat Taaffe were well aware of Christy's flaws and much later the jockey would admit that the horse's main problem at this stage of his career was the fact that he hurdled the big fences. 'He was a horse who really used to bend his hurdles,' he said, 'and when he hit one, he was so quick he could find a leg to save himself somehow. Unfortunately his head would disappear completely and, as he didn't have much of a neck, you'd find yourself with nothing at all in front of you, which was apt to be disconcerting to say the least. A remarkable horse,' he recalled.

Pat Samuel remembers that while the decision to run Christy in the Gold Cup did indeed cause a sensation in Ireland, he could not quite believe the reaction. 'I distinctly remember having told Pat before the race in Thurles that my wife and I wanted the horse to run in the Gold Cup. We already had an entry for it and for the novice race, but we wanted to run him in the big one. The thinking was that, in my experience of the horse world, there is no such thing as a horse "for next year". If you are too cautious then something always happens – the bloody horse breaks down or something. I told Pat that we should definitely go for it now while we have the horse. Aside from that I was always confident that we could beat the English horses and it has always been my opinion that if you're not confident, then you shouldn't involve yourself in steeplechasing. But I was still taken aback by the reaction to the decision we took. I mean the papers were basically saying that I was off my rocker because this was a good horse, but not that good. Certainly it was going to be a big jump up for Christy, but my motto has always been "have a go". I've done that with every bloody horse I ever had. If you've got a chance, have a go – that's what it's all about. If you don't try something, then you'll never know if it was possible.

'It was the same for me with the horse Grand Canyon, who we ran in four major races in eight weeks and we won them all and the horse broke the track record every time. When we said we were going to try it people said we were mad, but we were proved right to try it. We only achieved it because I wanted to have a go at it.'

Tos Taaffe reflects that while the decision might not have been one that many racing insiders expected, it was one which was nevertheless typical of the connections.

'It certainly was not the done thing to send a novice to the Gold Cup – it was certainly not convention then or now – but that tells you all you need to know about Pat Samuel and Pat Taaffe because they did things their own way. It was probably more typical of Pat [Taaffe] because he always felt he could go against the norms,' he comments.

According to the stable vet Jimmy Kelly, the decision to send Christy to the Gold Cup raised questions asked about running a novice, but he feels it was the right move.

'The thing was that Pat Taaffe did not have horses hanging around, he ran them and gave them plenty of it. How many of his horses jumped off and made the running in their races? Quite a lot of them did. That was his way – he liked to have them very fit. And if you have them very fit and if they stay, then they can run everything else into the ground.

'I must say that it was not really a surprise to me that they ran Christy in the Gold Cup as a novice. He ran well and generally he jumped well, so why not? Sure, the best of them will have their off days, when you think of it. But nothing Pat did surprised me and for him to send the horse to take on the best of the British horses certainly did not surprise me either. I felt that if someone like Pat Taaffe, with all the experience he had and having ridden in so many Gold Cups himself, if he thought the horse was good enough, then the horse was good enough. He was sitting up on him every day, so who, in the name of God, would contradict him. Nobody.'

Assessing the decision now, Pat Murphy reckons that the connections obviously got it right.

'The PZ Mower Chase in Thurles was a better trial than anything he had done in the novice races. I know Thurles never took a lot of jumping, but he went round there like a ballet dancer, apart from the last. There were some half-decent horses in that race and he still won it by nearly a fence and a half, never having come out of second gear.

'There was always the view, whether Pat thought it himself or whether it was pushed on him, that with jumpers there is always the fear of injury. So some would come to the view that if everything was all right with the horse – then why not. Plus the fact that Pat was never a fan of the Sun Alliance Chase, which was, of course, the alternative and which, to this day, many people don't like. More runners, less experience, going faster at the wrong time in the race – all those sorts of things put people off. In the Gold Cup there was only ever going to be ten or twelve runners, so there would be more room to manoeuvre. That was the thinking at the time – with fewer runners you were less likely to get blinded at a fence. Many novices have tried it since, but that year it was certainly not the case that "hey, we'll throw him in at the deep end because the Gold Cup looks weak". You could not say that now.

'After the PZ, the Gold Cup was definitely the way to go. I mean, the horse had done what many previous Irish challengers had done, but he did lack experience by comparison. I think the fact both of them had been there and done it, they were able to weigh that up against the ability this horse had. In fairness too, it must be remembered that Arkle had not a lot of experience of fences when he came to his first Gold Cup. Back then too, Arkle was still very fresh in people's minds and what Tom Dreaper had done with the horse was something I have no doubt played on Pat's mind. He would have been thinking throughout Christy's chasing career, "Well, what would Tom have done?"

'The Gold Cup was, as it still is, the pinnacle of jump racing and there is no doubt they were brave to go the way they did, even if they knew between them that they could well win it,' he says.

It would appear that there was a major sense of relief in Alasty at the decision and while everyone in the yard – not least Pat Taaffe – knew the Gold Cup was going to be a big ask, at least they now knew for certain the size of the challenge ahead and could plan accordingly.

It is almost certain too that Bobby was pleased at the decision and while he had nightmares about the two failures at Ascot and Haydock, there was an inevitable feel about himself and Christy taking on the Gold Cup challenge. Here, he felt, was a very obvious opportunity for professional and personal redemption, one which he could not allow to pass.

In the meantime, following his earlier injury scare, Bula reappeared on Saturday 2 March at Newbury when Fred Winter's second jockey, Johnny Francome, had the ride on the horse in the Geoffrey Gilbey Memorial Chase. But, even though he won comfortably against moderate opposition, Bula came out of the race lame.

A subsequent veterinary examination showed he had chipped a small piece of bone from the top of his pastern on the off-fore leg and he was now unlikely to make Cheltenham.

A further examination on the Monday after the race confirmed the worst and the horse's trainer declared, 'He will definitely not run again this season.'

And so it was that on Tuesday 12 March, seven runners were declared for the big race – Charlie Potheen, The Dikler, Pendil, Game Spirit, High Ken, Inkslinger and Captain Christy.

Bobby would, of course, ride Christy, but just days before the festival he paid another visit to Austin Darragh where he was the recipient of some very bad news. Bobby had been experiencing violent stomach cramps and a sensation of burning heat, which were a side effect of the Parentrovite injections. Darragh told him bluntly, 'Bobby, I can't give you any more. Your heart won't take it.' Bobby now knew that the Gold Cup would indeed be a last chance for him when it came to rubber-stamping his comeback.

The good doctor, who was no mean horseman himself, had also been studying Christy and his analysis led him to believe that Bobby must be at his absolute sharpest for the Gold Cup. 'You must go into very strict training and get yourself really tuned up, because this horse is so quick you must have the reflexes of a young man.'

Bobby knew his visit to his doctor meant his second career was pretty much over, but at least he had Christy to look forward to as well, of course, as Yenesei in the Champion Hurdle. The news was bad in some ways, but it also strengthened his resolve to go out on a high note.

On the other hand Christy's owners were similarly resolute and Pat Samuel was a man for whom the bookies held little fear and he had been assiduously backing Yenesei each way for the Champion Hurdle, as well as coupling him with Captain Christy for the Gold Cup in some monstrous each-way doubles.

To this end, Yenesei was deliberately ridden to be placed

in the Champion Hurdle and that is exactly what happened. The race, it was generally accepted beforehand, was a two-horse affair between Fred Winter's Lanzarote and Fred Rimell's Comedy Of Errors with Richard Pitman and Bill Smith the respective riders.

The experts were not wrong on this occasion and in the end it was Pitman who prevailed on Lanzarote by three lengths. Yenesei finished a further eight lengths back at the enormous price of 100/1, delighting all involved, apart from the glum Bobby who reflected afterwards that had he made more use of the New Zealand-bred, he might have finished closer. But, on the whole everyone was happy – especially Pat Samuel. Prior to the race Yenesei had been widely available at 50/1, but he drifted in the market before the off. In fact, the owner had backed him widely at 200/1 in the weeks and days leading up to the race and was absolutely thrilled with the result, even when Bobby told him that had the horse been ridden closer to the pace he could have won. 'Keep that to yourself,' he told the jockey.

But now the focus had moved on to the final day of the festival and what was, without doubt, the day of destiny for Bobby and Christy.

Christy – A Dream Champion

Thursday 14 March 1974 dawned bright and clear, which was a huge relief for Christy's connections, especially as earlier in the week snow had threatened to postpone the meeting altogether. Another bonus was that the mild weather had dried out the ground and the going was just on the soft side of good – perfect for the Irish horse.

In the run-up to the race the English would not hear of defeat and confidently expected either the title holder The Dikler or Pendil to win, with the latter being the choice of most experts. The Irish, on the other hand, always picked one of their own and on this occasion many racing writers liked the look of Dan Moore's Inkslinger, the American-owned and -bred seven-year-old.

In his Cheltenham preview in the *Sunday Press*, Tony O'Hehir had reckoned that 'Inky' would have the measure of both Pendil and The Dikler. He said the horse had been specifically trained for this race and, although he had never won over the Gold Cup trip and on the only occasion he had taken on the 3-miles-2-furlongs distance (in the Irish Grand National), he had been beaten into fourth place.

'But his battling qualities have been evident in races on both sides of the Atlantic,' O'Hehir maintained, 'and as a four-year-old he won the Colonial Cup – a two-mile-six-furlong chase run at a gallop that would make many a seasoned race-goer's hair stand on end.'

He picked Inkslinger to beat both Pendil and The Dikler, while also noting that Captain Christy had a trainer and rider steeped in Gold Cup tradition and if the horse 'had the class between the fences' his jumping was 'anything but reliable'.

Michael O'Farrell in *The Irish Times* was another to favour Dan Moore's horse and on the morning of the race he said that 'in the hope that near perfect ground will prevail today I put forward Inkslinger as the one most likely to topple Pendil in the Gold Cup'.

He reasoned that, ever since the American-bred horse won the Two Mile Champion Chase (now the Queen Mother Champion Chase) and the Cathcart Cup within forty-eight hours of each other at Cheltenham the previous year, Inkslinger had been prepared with the Gold Cup and only the Gold Cup in mind and the trainer reckons 'that Inkslinger has improved tremendously in the interim'.

O'Farrell said he accepted that Christy 'may negotiate these well-presented fences better than he has at home' and that the trainer and jockey 'believe he will go very close', but he made Inkslinger his nap.

In the *Irish Press*, Tony Power went against the grain – and tradition – by predicting that The Dikler would prevail. While noting Christy as the 'enigma of the race' who could go close if he jumped a clear round, he felt the strength and experience of Fulke Walwyn's eleven-year-old would be the telling factor.

Bobby himself would later recall that, in order to save expense, the owners had sent himself and Pat Taaffe to Cheltenham on a package trip, but that this, curiously, worked to their benefit. 'As the two of us were having breakfast in a strange hotel away from the usual racing crowd at the Queen's, we were able to have a lengthy open discussion of our tactics for the Gold Cup.

'I suggested, "Let's surprise them all by holding him up. They'll be expecting us to go on and they think we have very little chance in any case. He'll jump better settled. We know that he gets the trip and he has plenty of speed." Pat agreed that we should let him settle down, play it cool and have no set plan.'

Bobby reckoned that anyone who was at Prestbury Park on that auspicious day would never forget it. 'The weather was like mid-June,' he remembered, 'and, looking at the huge happy crowd and the sun-drenched hills in the background, I thought there is no more glorious place. Christy had travelled well and, despite the heat, he was as cool as any of the runners as we paraded in front of the stands.'

As Bobby strutted his remarkably calm charge he knew he had to erase all the bad memories – especially those relating to Ascot and Haydock – and also put from his mind the feelings of racing's 'experts' who believed his mount had no chance of winning.

Some people might realistically think that Bobby had every bit as much of a chance of getting into a stew before the start as his horse, but the reforming alcoholic was using every trick in the AA canon to put negative and useless thoughts from his mind at this most crucial stage of his professional and personal rehabilitation.

'I knew that, if I could organise him, Christy would win. It was a fresh start. I turned to canter down, completely relaxed and free from all pressures at last. It was up to me,' he later remembered of his pre-race feelings.

He wasn't the only one feeling confident. John Nicholson,

the son of the man who first purchased Christy, says that prior to the race he felt the horse would win too. 'At all stages on the day I felt Christy was on song and would win. I know there might have been sentiment involved, but I genuinely felt he would do it.'

For his part, Pat Samuel's recollection is that he was 'apprehensive' rather than worried about the horse. 'The main fear was that he wouldn't be good enough. I wasn't worried about it because all you can do is have a go and if you're lucky you win and if you're unlucky, you don't. For all that though, it was pretty amusing because Dickie Gaskell, Ladbrokes' rails representative, drove me up to Cheltenham and on the way I had a few more bets with him and he thought he was going to make a killing.'

Many racing fans, given the history of the Gold Cup, look to the previous year's renewal for pointers for the upcoming race and 1974 was no different. That being the case, the main focus of attention was on the battle between The Dikler and Pendil who had locked horns in 1973 with the former coming out on top.

Of that race, Pendil's jockey Richard Pitman recalls that he had been beaten by going too soon.

'The horse froze when he jumped the last,' he says. 'There is a huge amount of colour either side and to go up that Cheltenham hill is an amazing thing because there is this little ribbon of green sward which gets narrower into the distance and either side there is this huge blast of colour and noise. Not that you're listening to the noise, but it is there and on that occasion Pendil froze just for a stride or two and got caught by The Dikler; he did fight back and was only beaten by a head. He was ahead a stride after the line, but the bookies don't pay out for being ahead a stride after the line.

'That first year, Fred Winter and I talked it over and I told him that what I wanted to do was to make my move halfway up the run-in. He said, "Look Richard, you only get one Gold Cup and if the horse makes a mistake at the last, you will not recover and you will not get back. I would rather you were beaten by going too soon than coming too late." That was the decision. In the event we got beat.'

Pitman and Winter were determined the same thing would not happen again in 1974 and they were extremely confident that they had the measure of everything else in the field. That confidence was shared by both the specialist racing media and the racing public, to the point that Pendil was made the 13/8 on favourite for the big race.

Bobby's personal recollection of the 1974 Gold Cup is pretty terse, given the importance of the occasion and the potential effects – good and bad – of the outcome, but then Bobby was not given to hyperbole.

'Charlie Potheen jumped off in front with the rest of us bunched up behind at a moderate gallop. Coming down the hill for the first time I was about a length behind the American horse Inkslinger when he fell and so nearly brought me down. His hind legs caught Christy's forelegs and he stumbled badly, but he recovered and was jumping beautifully, nicely settled down.'

For his part, riding Pendil – the odds-on favourite for the second year running – Pitman was anxious that the previous year's beating was not going to be repeated.

'Pendil was a little horse and Christy was a long, strong horse, while The Dikler was even bigger and stronger and as the race went on I was jumping and pulling back, jumping and pulling back. In a Gold Cup, when you are coming down the hill for the last time, there are not many times when a jockey is on a horse that is running away. That was the case with me and I was thinking "whoa, come here". I was second coming down the hill behind High Ken who was a bad jumper and I knew that, even if people later accused me of being brainless. I knew exactly what High Ken was – a bad jumper. He was ridden by Barry Brogan and trained by John Edwards, but he was a bad jumper. My plan was that I had to anchor my horse because if I showed him daylight, then he was gone. I would hit the front too soon and get stuffed the same as the previous year.

'Anyway, I'm in behind a notorious jumper coming down the hill to that notorious fence in the dip and I'm thinking that I'll pull him out, let him ping the fence and then pull him back in behind High Ken again and get a lead down to the bottom bend. Both Bobby and Ron Barry could see what I was doing because they were behind us coming down to the third last. We were going at a rate of knots and they could see that my horse was running away with me, so what did they do? They came around the outside and they shut the door. There was no exit for me. All of a sudden, my plan evaporated into thin air. Going into the fence, all I could do was pray. "God, please just let us get over this fence." And it did not happen. High Ken fell and Pendil was tripped up, which was a major disappointment given that he'd never fallen in his life. When we finished rolling and the clatter and the noise had abated and the quiet descended, there was poor old Pendil looking around and obviously wondering "what the hell happened there?" I stood up and I could only barely hear the tannoy and it was all "Captain Christy and The Dikler are neck and neck and Captain Christy is going to get up".

'I had just had my world ripped apart for the second year running in the big race, but you feel for people and I felt for Bobby that day. It was marvellous. Bobby was a hero of mine. I knew what he'd been through and for him to come back then was truly the most marvellous thing.'

Terry Biddlecombe has always maintained that he shouted at Pitman to 'watch that f★★★★r' before High Ken came down. His reasons were perfectly rational, as he explains: 'High Ken was trained by John Edwards and I got worried about him because he was not jumping properly and I was definitely of the opinion that I was going to keep out of the way of that f★★★★r. Beasley pulled out for a bit of light, which was a very good move on his behalf and much like myself, he probably didn't like the look of the way High Ken was jumping. You try and weigh them up in a race, you know, and when you see them making mistakes you get very cautious. On the flat it is much different, of course, because you can get shut in. But if you are jumping well, then you can always go to the outside, get a bit of light and keep out of trouble. That way you get a clear run. That said, going around the outside at Cheltenham is not always the most recommended way, but Pat Taaffe used to do that and take them wide from the water jump and squeeze them up the hill to the last ditch to try and take more ground on the outside. It may look as if you're going wide, but you've got to try and get a clear run from there, otherwise you'll get shut in, which is a bugger.'

Pitman says he cannot recall if Biddlecombe had shouted something at him. 'If he did, I never heard it. I knew what I was following and I didn't need to be told. And, I would say, the way they closed the door when I tried to get out, I'd say they were all very happy with the outcome – even Biddlecombe, because he ended up in third place on Game Spirit.'

Bobby's recollection of the incident is pretty similar to that of his rival, but there is no indication that he and Ron Barry acted in tandem to pin Pendil in behind High Ken. 'As we turned for home at the top of the hill for the second and final time, I planned to sit behind The Dikler and Pendil until the last fence, knowing that we had the speed to beat them on the run-in. I had been tracking a horse called High Ken but, for some reason, I didn't like the look of him. My experience told me that when the tap was turned on down the hill, he might be a bit dodgy. So I moved to the outside.

'Sure enough he [High Ken] fell at the third last and brought down the favourite Pendil, who was tracking him. I heard the crash and realised to my dismay that, with Pendil gone, I now had only The Dikler to lead me to the last and he was not going quite fast enough. I cruised upsides Ron Barry [on board The Dikler] and Christy met the fence perfectly. I asked him ... and he put down, hitting the fence hard with his chest. Once again his head disappeared, but this time I was ready for him. I picked him up, balanced him and passed The Dikler on the run-in.'

To the millions watching on television, the last fence blunder was relayed to them by the satin-voiced Peter O'Sullevan. Hardly able to contain himself, he told his viewers, 'Captain Christy jumps the last and ... he's nearly down. He's nearly down and The Dikler regains the lead. The Dikler goes into the lead, but Captain Christy is fighting back. Captain Christy goes to the front again. Striding up to the line and Captain Christy is going to win the Gold Cup. At the line Captain Christy is the winner, The Dikler is second.'

Standing at the last fence that day was Ted Walsh and his memories of those moments are crystal clear, even now.

'I was standing at the last fence that day in the Gold Cup with a pal of mine, Eddie O'Connor from Killorglin. Christy hit it such a belt I thought he was gone. I couldn't get over that he stood up. He caught it low down in front, but he galloped on. He just didn't stab at it – he just galloped on. Beasley had a good hold of him and while Christy nodded out on his head, Bobby had enough to hold on to. He was a length ahead of Ron Barry and The Dikler at the fence and three strides after it, he was a length down, but he galloped on, got going, and got up to win. He was some gee-gee, that's all I can say.'

Pat Samuel maintains he was not too confident going into the race, although Pat Taaffe had told him to back the horse. 'It might have been the fact that I was not too involved in English racing that I was not so confident,' he says. 'I think Jane was quite confident, but I was only hopeful rather than expectant. I only backed the two horses each way.

'And when Pendil fell, I was still not that confident. We certainly had seen one of the dangers removed, but we still had to beat the previous year's winner.

'I certainly thought he'd fallen at the last fence and I remember Jane shouting at me, "He's down." Certainly if it had not been for Bobby sitting as tight as he did, we'd never have won. Watching the race it looked like the horse would come down and I still feel that if it had been an ordinary National Hunt jockey on him instead of a man like Beasley, the horse would have fallen.'

Watching from the sitting room at home in Alasty, Tom Taaffe says the tension was palpable. 'I remember watching the race and thinking he was going well enough throughout and going to the last it looked nailed-on that he'd win, but as we all know he walked through the last. I have to say at that point I assumed he was beaten. All the lads from the yard were in the sitting room with us and we all had our hearts in our mouths throughout the race. Everyone nearly died when he hit the last and it really was like watching a drama unfold and we couldn't believe it when Bobby got him together and beat The Dikler up the hill. It was quite ironic, many years later, when Kicking King rooted the last on the way to his King George. I was being interviewed afterwards and I was very blasé when saying "ah, sure, there is no point in hacking up in these races, you need a bit of drama and excitement'. I never actually mentioned it in the interview, but what was going through my head was Christy's last fence drama in the Gold Cup.'

Bobby remembered that the Cheltenham crowd sang 'When Irish Eyes Are Smiling' as he was led back into the winners' enclosure.

'The cheers as I rode in were deafening and very flattering because they came from thousands who lost their money and were applauding me personally. It was marvellous and I was very grateful.'

It might be hard to extract from these modest words the magnitude of what Bobby had achieved. He had just won the Blue Riband of National Hunt racing which is no mean feat in itself. But he had done so on board a novice horse while at the same time being a recovering alcoholic and pressing on in age. The significance was not lost on him, but he was not as overcome as he might have been; such an attitude could, after all, lead to regression, and regression was the last thing he needed after what he had been through.

But if he was not getting too carried away, the newspapers certainly were and Michael O'Farrell in the following day's *The Irish Times* was no exception.

'To the lustful strains of "When Irish Eyes Are Smiling", followed by three of the heartiest cheers ever heard at Cheltenham, the Pat Taaffe-trained 7-year-old novice Captain Christy and his 38-year-old rider, the indomitable Bobby Beasley, were greeted in the unsaddling enclosure after winning yesterday's Gold Cup by five ground devouring lengths from last year's winner The Dikler with Game Spirit trailing home a remote third,' he reported.

'Beasley, who steered Roddy Owen to win back in 1959, gave his mount a superb ride from behind to take on the gigantic The Dikler after the third last fence where High Ken brought down Pendil. Stride for stride the two cleared the next jump, but rising to the final fence Captain Christy had his rival's measure, albeit he pitched on landing leaving The Dikler to wrest a slight lead beginning the run-in.

'However, Beasley let his mount settle and in a few strides had headed The Dikler again before sweeping up the hill to a magnificent triumph – the first chaser in his first season to lift the Gold Cup since Mont Tremblant twenty-two years ago.

'What would have happened had Pendil not been brought down at the third last is anybody's guess, but judging by last year's result when only inches separated The Dikler and Pendil, Captain Christy must have won. "Believing that he had more speed than both Pendil and The Dikler we decided to wait with Captain Christy for the first time, he never came from so far behind before," said Taaffe, who was saddling his first Gold Cup winner but rode four himself. "Bobby gave him a super ride," he added. "But now I want Captain Christy to equal Golden Miller's record of five Gold Cups."

'As the horse only had six runs over fences and failed to finish the course in two previous races in England, Taaffe would have preferred to run Captain Christy in the Sun Alliance Chase on Tuesday, but on the insistence of his owner Mrs Samuel, he was prepared for yesterday's big race. Mrs Samuel collected £30,000 for a £1,000 each-way bet with Ladbrokes.

'For once Captain Christy jumped really well as he waited behind the field and I only saw him make two slight errors, at the fence before the water and at the last.

'Taaffe lavished praise on Captain Christy when he added "I've always said he was the best chaser I've ever sat on apart from Arkle." Beasley, who staged such a great comeback after leaving racing for a couple of years, said, "Absolutely wonderful. The 'Captain' got a bit close to the last one, but I was ready for him."

'Fulke Walwyn said, "I cannot believe it. When Pendil went I thought The Dikler was there and I still thought we would win at the last. The winner is a brilliant horse when he jumps and he jumped today."

'Ron Barry said, "I have no excuses. Captain Christy beat me fair and square for speed from the last.' Richard Pitman said, "I'm disappointed. Pendil was running away. I was right behind High Ken when he fell and brought me down."'

O'Farrell's excitement was reflected across the Irish media as hacks desperately tried to fill out this miraculous story. It emerged that the trainer and the jockey had 'shared the schooling' of the horse and this was a critical factor, according to Pat Taaffe.

Bobby also said the victory was a 'tribute to persistent schooling' and that he and Pat Taaffe had had 'a real psychological battle' with the horse. 'We had to give him intensive schooling at jumping to make him forget about hurdle racing and get him to steady and jump like a chaser. I was schooling him in my sleep.'

He also said that the Gold Cup was the first time Christy had been ridden from behind in a steeplechase and this was undoubtedly a factor in his upsetting the odds. 'We decided today that I would ride him like a racehorse, hold him up, and use his speed.'

Tom McGinty's analysis in the *Irish Independent* said that the credit had to go to both Bobby and Pat Taaffe. Bobby, he said, was, five years ago, a 13½ stone insurance salesman who had fought his way back from the wilderness, while Pat Taaffe had been the architect of 'a stiff programme, a subject of much wry comment before yesterday, that made this astounding triumph possible'.

Admiration for the achievement was not exclusive to the Irish racing media and much later Bobby's friend and foe Terry Biddlecombe would express a view which was echoed by many in the racing game. 'Christy was the last novice to win it and I must say I cannot remember too much talk beforehand about the wisdom of bringing a novice to the Gold Cup, but Bobby gave him a brilliant ride. I cannot actually say I saw the incident where Bobby nearly came down at the last because I was too busy trying to keep my fellow going. But it was a great riding performance and he really excelled himself on the day. Sure, he was afraid he'd make a balls of it on the day, but he was such a good horseman he was able to carry it off. He really did the job.'

Back at Alasty, there was understandable joy and no little drama, as Tom Taaffe recollects, 'I watched the race at home in Alasty and I remember one of the girls got so excited when Christy made his famous blunder at the last that she accidentally got a knitting needle stuck in her hand. It was very dramatic, between one thing and another.'

His sister Olive was stuck at boarding school, but got to see the race. 'I watched the race at school and I can't remember if I had to mitch off a class or what, or was the race late enough that classes were over, but I saw it in the common room at school. I don't remember having to get any special time off class or even getting into any trouble for it, but that was where I saw it. I remember a few things about it, particularly the last fence.'

The victory also hit the Irish front pages the following day, reflecting the level of interest throughout the country in the fortunes of the intrepid trio. On the *Irish Independent's* front page story, under the headline 'Great win for Pat Taaffe' and alongside a picture clearly illustrating the near capsize at the last fence, the paper reported that 'the greatest Irish roar since the days of Arkle' had erupted at Cheltenham when Captain Christy crossed the line.

Similarly, the *Irish Press* said, 'It was Ireland's day at Cheltenham yesterday. Captain Christy, trained by Pat Taaffe and ridden by Bobby Beasley, stunned cross-channel critics by winning the Gold Cup and was given the kind of reception Arkle got when he completed his hat-trick in the jumping classic.' The story also reported that Pat Taaffe had become only the second man to ride and train a winner of the Gold Cup; the first was Danny Morgan, for whom Bobby had ridden Roddy Owen back in 1959.

Later in the week the various commentators in the *Irish Field* also ran the rule over the victory, with Neville Ring on the front page describing the race as 'one of the most dramatic Gold Cups of all time', concluding that as Christy's fencing prior to the race had been so hair-raising 'Pat Taaffe and Bobby Beasley have worked miracles', while Bobby himself 'deserved to be the happiest man at Cheltenham, as he has returned to the top of his profession'.

Jonathan Powell, in his 'English Notebook' column headlined 'Beasley triumphs in battle of bulge' said there were a host of stories to tell in the wake of the race, but none could match the crowning glory of Bobby's 'incredible' comeback.

'A few years ago, as all Ireland knows, he returned home after giving up a top retainer in England, sickened by the ceaseless battle against the scales,' he said, ignoring the fact that Bobby's battle had been more with the bottle than with the weighing scales.

'The man who had graced British racing retired prematurely to become an insurance salesman and it seems only two or three years ago since he turned up at Cheltenham weighing something like 13½ stone and looking about as happy as a fox in Piccadilly Circus.

'Beasley's own determination was the decisive factor in his decision to try again and, with the help of staunch support from his friends, Bobbie [sic] set about re-launching his career as a jockey. The odds were stacked against him, the battle was grim and progress at first seemed painfully slow. But gradually Irish trainers realised the man could still ride; the touch was as sure as ever and the will to win, forged in the lean times, perhaps greater than ever before.

'Talking over the race outside the Cheltenham weighing room on Thursday, Bobbie acted with all the obvious delight of a man who has been to the brink [a nod to the obvious] and has seen only too clearly what is on the other side.

'"I am very lucky to be here," he smiled, but he alone made it possible. Was he worried when Captain Christy hit the last fence hard? "Not really, I was ready for him to do it. You see he has been doing it very often this season, but I did let my leathers down a hole or two today."'

Powell's piece, while not really spelling out the facts, did give people some idea of what the victory meant to Bobby and what he had come through to achieve it, but it would still be some years before his battle with the drink became common knowledge.

In the hours and days following the race, there was much talk – most of it from England – that had Pendil stood up and not been brought down by High Ken, then he would have won. One of the most vocal racing insiders in this regard was none other than Lord John Oaksey, the aristocrat and racing journalist who was formerly a very successful amateur jockey.

That being so, Pat Samuel called him up and asked him, 'Why would you say something silly like that?' He further told him that 'Pendil is not as good a horse as you make him out. He doesn't stay to start with.'

'Anyway, I suggested to him that we would have a match race over 3,000 metres at Kempton, which was Pendil's favourite track, and we would each put up £10,000. He said he could not afford to do that and I said, "Oh, well, then we won't do it." Then he said that Pendil would win the following King George and, of course, Christy destroyed him, as he would with Bula the following year after that.'

Even today Pat Samuel reckons that Pendil was indeed a top class chaser, but he believes he would have taken the money off Lord Oaksey had the match ever taken place.

Of course, Pat Samuel was a lot wealthier as a result of Christy's endeavours – especially when considering that many of his bets had involved each-way doubles with Yenesei.

'I got £178,000 when the each-way double bets came up and Ladbrokes actually asked me if I'd like to buy a stake in the company,' he says impassively. That was a massive amount of money back in 1974.

The horse's victory in the Gold Cup was one which was celebrated all over Ireland, not least in Johnstown, County Kilkenny, where John Nicholson reports that his family and friends 'partied for weeks afterwards, like we still owned the horse'.

One man who was most certainly not celebrating on the night of the race – or any night thereafter – was Bobby and, in fact, his return to Ireland after the Gold Cup victory was more low-key than even he might have planned, as Tony O'Hehir recalls.

'The flight we were on from Birmingham to Dublin was diverted to Shannon,' he says. 'I was meant to be commentating at the Phoenix Park or the Curragh the next day, but we ended up in a hotel in Limerick and I shared a hotel room with him that night. Bobby was very quiet about what had happened at Cheltenham and I remember we just chatted about old times. He certainly wasn't reliving the race or anything like that, but instead was talking about life in general and his times with Paddy Sleator and his old days in racing. He wasn't wittering on about races he should have won or anything like that, just talking about old times. In the end, I think he rode at Limerick the following day.'

Such were the vicissitudes of the racing game, but it was a game with which Bobby was becoming increasingly tired.

That was definitely not the case for Pat Samuel. Some time after the Gold Cup win, he got a call from an unexpected source.

'After the race – a couple of weeks after the race – I was having tea with the Queen Mother and she told me I was so lucky to have won the Gold Cup. She said she'd been trying her whole life to win the race and there was me winning it with a novice. "Bobby Beasley did a wonderful job riding him," she told me. I responded in the affirmative – that he had indeed done an excellent job, and she added, "If any other jockey had been on Christy at that last fence, you would not have won it." She did say that to me, so that was high praise indeed for Bobby. I think she knew more about jump racing than most.

'I actually knew her quite well and I bought a horse for her once. Once she sent a page around to my house with a letter inviting me to come and see her at Clarence House, so I went around to see her for lunch. She was very welcoming and asked me would I like a drink before eating and, of course, I accepted. I thought she'd ping a bell and someone would come along and take the order, but no, she went over to the drinks cabinet and asked me what I'd like. I said "I'd like a Dubonnet, your Majesty" and she decided she'd have the same.'

'Mr Samuel, it is very kind of you to come and see me,' the Queen Mother told him. 'I want you to do me a great favour. I want you to select a couple of horses for me in New Zealand.'

Pat's response was that this was very dangerous territory for a colonial like him as he might end up in the Tower of London if he messed up.

The Queen Mother smiled and said, 'Mr Samuel, I don't think we do that any more.'

Anyway, he bought her one horse and it was pretty decent. 'He ran well in his first novice hurdle – he hadn't been hurdling before, but he was the right type – to come second,' Pat Samuel recalls. 'In the next race he broke a leg in between fences and that was the end of that. Then I gave her a very good horse I had, but when he got to England he was on the way to the gallops one morning when he slipped on cobblestones in Lambourn and bust his hip. That was the end of him.'

Heady times indeed for Christy's owner.

When Bobby Left Christy

Shirley Beasley reckons that she did not see Bobby for some time after his big race triumph. 'I didn't see Bobby for three or four days after the Gold Cup – he never came home,' she revealed many years later. She may not have admitted it to herself back then, but with the benefit of hindsight she now realises she felt uneasy about the situation, possibly because of her suspicion that Bobby might have had his eye on someone else.

Her antennae were finely tuned at this stage of their relationship and she put a lot of store in her instincts. She knew Bobby better than he did and she could sense things in his demeanour.

'I said to Nicky Rackard one day, "I know he's got a woman up on the Curragh somewhere." He said, "You know enough, Shirley. You know enough."'

She says she did not know then who this other woman was – not until much later. 'I must admit that I knew Bobby had ridden a horse called Alaska Fort for Mick O'Toole and it seemed like he knew everything about the stable and I was left wondering why.'

It later turned out that the woman who would be Bobby's

second wife, Linda, worked for Mick O'Toole as his stable secretary.

This was going on while preparations were being made for Christy's next target after Cheltenham, the Irish Grand National at Fairyhouse on Monday 15 April, and in his *Irish Times* preview of the race, Michael O'Farrell made some further interesting observations about the Cheltenham win.

'Blest with unusual foresight or sheer good luck, owner Mrs Jane Samuel insisted that Captain Christy take his chance in last month's Gold Cup. That decision initiated an unorthodox crash programme designed to transform the highly impetuous novice into a sensible and settled racing machine. To the incredulity of most professionals the gambit paid off and horse, trainer and jockey basked in the tumultuous accolade accorded them in Cheltenham's unsaddling enclosure.'

He also wrote that only firm ground would have prevented Captain Christy from lining up today and 'such ground which impairs his action seemed likely to prevail, that is until the rains of last Wednesday night and Thursday ensured reasonable jumping conditions. The Samuel luck is holding.'

If the Samuel luck was holding until then, it vanished just seven fences into the Grand National when Christy and Bobby parted company in spectacular fashion. In glorious sunshine and in front of a massive bank holiday crowd, the ten runner field set off with Bobby lobbing Christy, who was carrying a massive 12 stone 2 lbs and conceding 14 lbs to the rest of the field, along at the rear of the field. The horse was jumping perfectly until he got too close to the seventh and paid what Tony Power described as 'the inevitable penalty'.

The finish was fought out between Jim Dreaper's Colebridge and Dan Moore's L'Escargot, despite the loose Christy causing the leaders a bit of bother, and it was Colebridge who eventually prevailed by five lengths.

A pragmatic Pat Taaffe said afterwards that Christy's fall was a racing incident and there was nothing to be done except swallow the disappointment and look forward. 'I will look at him in the morning and if the experience has not stiffened him up, I might run him in the Powers Gold Cup. It all depends on how he is.'

A possible explanation for the fall was offered by Bobby's weighroom colleague John Harty who told Tom McGinty of the *Irish Independent* after the race that he had walked the track the previous day at the same time the National would be run and he discovered a potential problem.

'I for one could not find the heart to question the shaken Beasley subsequently, but another experienced jockey, John Harty, told me that when he walked the course at approximately the same time the previous evening he noted how the sun cast a shadow at the fence in question making it difficult for the inexperienced horse to judge his take-off point,' McGinty reported the following morning.

Just as punters were reading the report with their breakfast, Pat Taaffe and his staff were evaluating Christy's 'morning after' demeanour and, happy with what he saw, the trainer packed the horse onto the transporter for a second trip to Fairyhouse.

Pat Murphy recalls that it was the horse himself who made the decision rather than his trainer or anyone else.

'We were all very downbeat when the horse fell that day, but I do remember the following morning, Pat had the horse out and he was as fresh as paint,' he says. 'So the decision [to run in the Powers Gold Cup] was made by the horse himself. Pat didn't seem to have any qualms about it at all and it wasn't as if he had run for five miles around Fairyhouse or anything. In fact, Christy being Christy, he ran as far as the paddock gate and stopped – typical. As for the fall itself, again Pat was not concerned. 'Horses fall for whatever reason and it might have been that he was blinded for a stride and was a little too long at the fence or even a little too short. These things happen and Pat did not seem concerned about it in any way, shape or form.'

Unfortunately in sport there are down sides as well as up and walking back to the weighroom after his fall Bobby encountered several disgruntled punters who had obviously backed Christy. Bobby's rehabilitation and subsequent Gold Cup win had gladdened the sporting heart of the Irish nation, but some are never satisfied and several people at Fairyhouse that day decided that Bobby was in some way to blame for Christy's fall. One even accused him of jumping off the horse.

Given Bobby's fragile temperament, listening to this was going to provoke a reaction one way or another. The best way he could find to shut them up was to ride Christy to victory in the Powers Gold Cup.

That was exactly what he did. Facing familiar rivals such as Lough Inagh and Perpol, he demolished them over the 2¼ mile trip, having started as the 4/5 favourite.

The *Irish Field*'s Dave Baker later reported that Christy had 'leaped well and sometimes brilliantly' to win by fifteen lengths with Perpol in second and Tarquin's Rose in third. Lough Inagh, apparently, had such a difficult time trying to keep up with Christy that jockey Sean Barker was unseated at the final fence by the fatigued horse.

All the talk in the papers was of Christy being put out to grass for the summer after his daring novice campaign and as the horse was the winner of six of his nine chases, Tom McGinty in the *Irish Independent* reckoned that Christy deserved the break – as did Taaffe and Beasley.

'He has been a tantalising horse in many ways,' McGinty

said. 'The Gold Cup and yesterday's performance to a lesser degree have shown us just how brilliant he is capable of being, but his frequent lack of respect for even the stiffest of obstacles, although an indication of his courage, remains a problem to be ironed out before next season.'

However, if all seemed well in the light of this latest victory, it was far from being so. Bobby remembers how, as he was leaving the parade ring before the race, he was on the receiving end of more abuse from a segment of the crowd.

'All the adulation of Cheltenham was forgotten,' he recounted. 'I was roared and booed by people who seemed convinced that I had deliberately engineered that fall [in the Irish Grand National] and I asked myself "what is it all about?" This is a load of rubbish. I've done what I set out to do. Living is more important than racing and it's time to get out.'

The incident went largely unnoticed in the media, apart from a section of the late, great Micheál O'Hehir's column in the *Sunday Press* the following week.

Under the headline 'Contempt for Yahoos' O'Hehir wrote he had nothing but disdain for those yahoos who 'spoiled the great Fairyhouse meeting' for many.

'There were a handful of no-gooders who abused rider Bobby Beasley, not just when he came in after the Irish Grand National in which he was a casualty, but also the following day when he was going out on the same horse for the Powers Gold Cup,' O'Hehir reported.

'These individuals (imagine thinking of them as sportsmen!) hurled abuse at the rider telling him how to ride and "not fall off" in what was a most despicable manner.

'Bobby Beasley has won Cheltenham Gold Cups, an Aintree Grand National and hundreds of other races. The man is bred for jockeying and no man has worked at his calling harder than he and few have achieved the success he has. To subject a man to this type of low abuse is beyond reason,' he wrote.

There is no doubting the effect this had on Bobby. His fragile temperament was too delicate for that carry-on. Pat Murphy believes that the boorish behaviour probably amounted to nothing more than sore punters venting their frustration. 'The thing with Bobby getting abuse at Fairyhouse is that you will always get people talking through their pockets and if he did get a lambasting from the crowd, it was more than likely because they backed Christy and didn't like him being beaten and them losing their money.'

Even so, it did have a marked effect on the jockey and it is fair to say that a combination of factors — Austin Darragh's diagnosis on his health, the increasingly hopeless state of his marriage, the Gold Cup victory and the abuse he received at Fairyhouse — all combined to make Bobby's mind up for him. It was time to retire.

In keeping with his often extremely curious character, however, he did not bother telling anyone. For Pat Taaffe in particular, especially given the faith he had shown in Bobby, this was a very disappointing turn of events.

A Parting of the Ways and a Sad Ending

C hristy and Bobby went their separate ways. Of course, both had other successes – Christy went on to win two King Georges, while Bobby continued his battle against the drink and had a happy second marriage – but for the rest of their lives they would remain public property as one of the greatest partnerships in racing history.

While both Bobby and Pat Samuel found contentment in later life, Pat Taaffe and Christy had great successes but much sadness as well and these two great figures of National Hunt racing would not end their days as they or many other people would have liked.

Immediately after the Powers Gold Cup, Bobby decided to end his career in the saddle and he also decided to end his marriage. For Shirley Beasley this was a relief in many ways, but there was still a lot of pain to be endured as the separation process gathered momentum.

Although she knew of Linda's existence at that stage and her place in her husband's life, she maintains she was only too glad to put the disastrous marriage behind her.

'All I know is that he told me he wanted a divorce or a

separation, or whatever. Quite frankly I had had enough at that stage and I said, "Fair enough, you go to your solicitor first.'"

Shirley maintains that the first time they split up she knew she had to get out to protect herself and her children. However, 'like a bloody fool', she was persuaded back into Bobby's life for a short while.

'I listened to all the promises and everything, but it was no good. When Linda came on the scene – I knew he had this girlfriend – I just hoped he'd hang on to her long enough [for me] to get a separation. I told him to go to his solicitor first of all and then I went to mine. You had to stay in the same house to get a legal separation – it was awful in Ireland thirty-five years ago in that regard – and while he disappeared for days at a time, I was not bothered by then. It was quiet when he disappeared.

'Then we had our day in court and I just moved back down here [to her parents' house in Wexford] and she moved in there [to Bobby's farm] the same day. He was storming around the house before I left – "when are you going to go?" I later heard she was waiting in Carnew to come down. Now I've nothing against her – the marriage was well and truly over by then. We just couldn't carry on the way it was.'

Shirley has no idea how Linda coped with Bobby as time went on, but she speculates that the new woman in his life was facing into a trying period. 'I would bet money she did not have an easy time with him early on; maybe it was not too bad later on when the fight was gone out of him,' she says.

Whether or not that was the case, Bobby and Linda lived happily until Bobby's death in 2008. Initially they lived in Wexford on Bobby's farm, but later moved to England.

Looking back on the remainder of Bobby's life, Linda says that, despite his sporting legend, it was his successful battle against the drink which made him most proud.

'I think he viewed conquering alcohol as being his biggest achievement,' she says, 'but I also believe the fact he won the Gold Cup on Captain Christy meant he was able to tangibly demonstrate that victory over alcohol to a wider public.

'Bobby was never terribly demonstrative, but to him winning the Gold Cup was proof to the world that he had overcome his problems. But certainly he felt that beating the drink was his greatest achievement.

'I mean, it is funny because he had a very reactive metabolism, if I can put it that way; in later life he reacted to certain medications and I think in some ways the alcohol was just another one of those. He didn't actually drink until he was twenty-four and I think there were those who egged him on, saying "ah come on, you're not a man unless you can take a drink" and that sort of thing. The problem then seemed to accelerate quite quickly and although I was not around, I certainly get the feeling that is what happened.'

Bobby's widow says she does not know if the incident at Fairyhouse where he was so raucously badgered by the crowd contributed to his decision to stop riding and she feels that it was more to do with the fact that he was not getting many rides.

'Between that and the constant battle against the weight – he had to spend a terrific amount of time in the sauna keeping the weight off – and I think, really and truly, he felt that unless he could get a decent retainer, it was no longer worth his while. I think that had more to do with his retiring the second time than anything else,' she maintains, adding that the Gold Cup was the pinnacle for him and after that he never really had the appetite for it any more.

'I can remember him going to Roscommon to ride something at one point that summer and he really felt it wasn't worth the effort any more. He could have handed in his licence immediately after the Gold Cup, but I suppose it was a very difficult decision for him to make given that he had missed out on the best years of his life as a jockey. In the end I don't think the idea of driving to Roscommon for one ride which had no chance of winning really appealed to him that much. He would have been coming to the end of his career anyway,' she reckons.

On Monday 7 October 1974, Bobby's retirement was made official. *The Irish Times* reported, 'From his farm in Wexford last night 39-year-old jump jockey Bobby Beasley said he was handing in his licence today and will not ride in public again. Beasley first retired five years ago after riding more than seven hundred winners, including Roddy Owen in the Gold Cup, Nicolaus Silver in the Grand National and Another Flash in the Champion Hurdle. He made a comeback in 1971 and partnered Captain Christy to victory in the Irish Sweeps Hurdle the following year and the Gold Cup last March. Beasley said, "I have no definite plans at the moment and will devote my time for the moment to the farm. I'm not keen about going along to meetings merely as a spectator. If I ever return to the sport I would like it to be as an assistant to some trainer in Ireland or England."'

Commenting on Bobby's decision, Ted Walsh reckons the whole thing was distinctly unusual. 'It was a terribly odd situation, when he finished. But then, he was an odd man and I would say that he could not have taken much stick or abuse.'

After announcing his decision Bobby trained in Ireland on his own farm, as Linda recalls. 'There was about 30 acres on the farm, so we didn't really have the proper facilities, but we had a few winners with moderate horses. Tom Conroy, who was a long-standing friend and who lived close by, sent us a couple of horses and they turned out to be pretty decent. We won a bumper with Master Velvet at Navan and a horse called

Serpent Three won a couple of hurdle races. We were actually going to go to Liverpool with him, but Tom was speaking to the postman who didn't think he had any chance, so he decided we couldn't go. Bobby was not terribly amused.'

Training in Ireland was not for Bobby and he and Linda decided to return to the UK and try their hand there.

'We moved to England around '79 or '80 and we trained for a while at both Lewes and Marlborough and again it was with moderate horses and was quite a struggle. He was a little frustrated by that, but he did enjoy it. He certainly enjoyed being with the horses and that side of things, but in the end you've got to be practical. It was certainly the case that he had had a lifetime with horses and wasn't really qualified for much else, but we decided we would look at small "free house" pubs and try and learn that business. In a way, that was another opportunity for Bobby to prove his point. Curiously, working in that environment there was never any temptation for him – nothing like that. In fact, he used to try and help people who came into the pub and who obviously did have a problem with drink. He'd try and counsel them a bit. But it was a remarkable thing to do – to be surrounded by booze and not feel threatened by it,' she said.

It is said that, during his time as a publican, Bobby would come into the bar every morning and throw a scornful eye along the line of optics and mutter, 'You bastards, you thought you were going to get me but you won't.'

Subsequently, Bobby struck up a working relationship with Linda Jewell, a young trainer based near Maidstone in Kent and according to his widow, working with Linda was a very happy time for him as it enabled him to get back with the horses, to go racing and to be involved.

'The horses never really left him and I suppose for all

sportsmen there is a challenge when they give up their profession because there is nothing that can ever really replace it,' she points out. 'He thoroughly enjoyed his time there and got great satisfaction from helping the young lads and lasses with their riding. He got a huge kick out of that and he also got a big kick helping Karen Jewell, Linda's daughter. She's a very tidy rider and she had some rides on the flat and over hurdles and won a couple of them. There was another young lad in the yard, Craig Messenger, who Bobby was very fond of and who he helped a lot. He had very close connections with Linda and he helped her as much as he was able. It was very much a mutually beneficial thing for both of them.'

Another person Bobby would encounter in this period of his life was Pat Murphy, the lad at Alasty during the Christy years who had subsequently gone on to become a successful trainer in his own right in England. The pair used to meet on a regular basis at southern tracks like Plumpton, Folkestone, Brighton, Fontwell and Salisbury and Pat says he used to enjoy those occasions, not only for the chance to reflect on their shared past, but also to hear Bobby's rich vein of racing stories.

Reflecting on Bobby's decision to retire when he did, Pat Murphy says it is perfectly understandable.

'I can say it now, looking back, but I could not have said it all those years ago, that the fact is Bobby was obviously in a fragile state of mind. Any sportsman or woman can get flak – huge flak – and they'll go to the pub, have a few drinks with their mates and forget about it. Bobby couldn't do that and he was probably on his own, stewing over what had happened and the public reaction to it. I remember, at the time, Pat being asked about Bobby and replying that he had not been able to contact him. But, Pat being Pat, he never stood in judgement over anyone. I think he was waiting for Bobby to contact him after a while and it just didn't happen. It was a very sad ending, second time around, to a career which obviously still had a lot to offer. Only Bobby knew, though, exactly how much it had to offer. And the fact that he just slipped quietly away into the background was a little bit sad. I still feel, though, that there was pressure at that time coming from somewhere. Maybe the owners hadn't been happy – and if that was the case, Pat certainly would have said it to Bobby. Or maybe Bobby himself felt there was a lack of faith in him, but the one thing I'll promise you is that the lack of faith did not come from Pat Taaffe. It may well have come from the owners.

'As we now know, there was obvious media pressure and while the media spotlight then might not have been as intense as it now is, the irony is that the papers back then carried more racing than they do now. Jockeys might get a bit of stick in the *Racing Post* these days, but back then they got it in every paper the length and breadth of the country – and on to the English papers. And the thing was that anyone who read a newspaper knew about what was going on. On top of that, with a horse like Christy, everyone wanted to know what was going on. Maybe it was that after winning the Gold Cup and then encountering the big failure in the Irish National – a huge high followed by a massive low – Bobby might have felt more pressure, even at that stage in his life, than he, as a person, felt he could handle. And maybe going home after Fairyhouse, he felt to himself that that was as far as it was going to go: enough was enough.'

Murphy's point about the owners showing a lack of faith in Bobby is a pertinent one. In his own book Bobby highlights the fact that the Samuels had initially offered him a retainer to ride their horses, but he insists they reneged on it.

'At first in the euphoria of Cheltenham I had been offered a retaining fee of one thousand pounds to ride Christy in the following season,' he wrote. 'I had accepted this because this would go a long way towards paying a cowman for my expanding dairy herd. Even when the offer was reduced to five hundred pounds, I reluctantly agreed to carry on for the sake of Pat and the horse, but when the owners said they couldn't afford this, I decided that the time had come to call it a day and to look after the cows myself.'

Whatever about that, his second retirement was one which was welcomed by his former weighroom colleagues Willie Robinson, Richard Pitman and Terry Biddlecombe, each of whom was overwhelmed by the fact he was ever able to have a second career at all.

'When it all fell apart for him, it was all very sad, especially as he was such an iconic figure to people like myself,' Pitman maintains. 'Then when he came back it was brilliant and doesn't that make it all the more meritorious that he could then kill that demon. There is no better way of going out than signing off with a win. It shows you the mettle of the man – he obviously just said to himself "the hell with it". It is a bit like when you are not going well in a race and you're thinking to yourself "I'll just jump one more and I'll pull up". Why one more? What's the point? That last one is the one that will break your neck or the horse's neck. Bobby was very clever in that decision. And I doubt very much if that was a spur of the moment decision, you know. He obviously thought to himself he had no more to prove. In reality he had nothing more to prove anyway, but people always seem to feel they have. I used to see him afterwards when I was working at the races and it would usually be at Fontwell or Plumpton, places like that, and he was such a gentle person. But invariably his first comment to you would be along the lines of "I'm still off it" or "I've beaten it" and it seemed to me that he was more proud of having beaten the devil drink than any of his racing exploits. I think that is the measure of the man. He was an alcoholic, but he beat it and what better thing could he do?'

Willie Robinson could never be described as one of Bobby's biggest fans, but he clearly understands the redemptive force of what he achieved. 'He'd come out of a very bad time,' Robinson maintains, adding, 'but I thought the comeback was the most fantastic thing that happened to anyone. It did not make him a better person in my view, but it certainly showed the strength of character that he had just to pull it off. He had lost his nerve and then he regained it again. How? I simply do not know.'

Bobby's old number two at Rimell's and a man with whom he had shared many a drink in the good-old-bad-old days, Terry Biddlecombe, was similarly impressed. 'It was a surprise to me and many of his colleagues that Bobby was able to come back from the problems he had – very much so. He had been in a hole; a big hole.

'He was, of course, a wonderful horseman – not in the same way as McCoy or Carberry these days – but he was able to get in behind his horse and he rode very long. He also had wonderful hands and was able to get his horse to settle. He also had a very good judge of pace and I think that could be put down to the fact that he rode for Paddy Sleator and when he used to ride his horses, most of the time he'd piss up on them. He was a great waiting jockey and had great patience.

'He had his ups and downs with many people – myself included – but he was a great man to ride with and we had a lot of laughs. He was a very exciting man whose life turned away from him, but it was lovely to see him come back and win such a big prize. That was his redemption.'

Bobby passed away on 9 January 2008. His funeral service was held at St Nicholas Church, Sandhurst, on 25 January and was attended by many racing luminaries.

★

For Pat Taaffe and Christy, Bobby's defection was, of course, a blow: the man who had put so much time and effort into making Christy a superstar and who understood the horse's uniquely flawed genius was gone. If this was an unwelcome turn of events, there was nothing to be done about it, except to carry on.

Bobby Coonan, who had ridden Christy in his second ever race under Pat Taaffe's care, was engaged to take over from Bobby and he rode the horse in fourteen of the fifteen races left in his career. Pat Taaffe announced to the newspapers that 'Bobby Coonan will ride Captain Christy in the Punchestown Free Handicap Chase on 24 October, the Black and White Gold Cup at Ascot and then in defence of the Gold Cup at Cheltenham.'

In fact, the plan didn't quite work that way and while Christy did run at Punchestown (unplaced) in late October, he was then sent back to Cheltenham rather than Ascot to run in the Massey-Ferguson Gold Cup on 7 December. It was not a successful venture as once again the horse was unplaced. What was to follow, however, was another eye-popping Captain Christy performance.

Pat Murphy was still in the yard at Alasty and he recalls the build-up to the King George VI Chase at Kempton on 26 December 1974.

'The season following his Gold Cup win was a tough one for the horse because obviously at that time there really were only handicaps open to him as there weren't as many conditions chases as there are nowadays. So Christy was invariably carrying up to twelve stone seven pounds in handicaps against younger horses to whom he was conceding lumps of weight. Those races were always going to be very difficult to win and, if you like, each of the races the following season was a stepping stone to Kempton — races the horse needed to run in. It was all experience and, of course, Bobby Coonan was only getting to know him and getting to know the ins-and-outs of him, which, as we know, were many and varied. Not always was it the case that what you learned in one race would stand you in good stead in the following one. There were lots of things like that and the season after he won the Gold Cup and the Powers Gold Cup was a tough one for him — until the King George when he put up a fantastic performance,' he recalls.

And what a fantastic performance it was. The race was billed as a duel between Christy and Pendil, the horse which the English racing fraternity maintained should have won the previous season's Gold Cup. To most of the English racing corps Pendil was the 'automatic choice' and his starting price for the race reflected that as he was 2/1 on as against the 5/1 being offered against Christy winning.

The headlines the day after the race summed up what had happened at Kempton rather succinctly: 'Captain Christy Thrashes Pendil' (*The Irish Times*) was a fairly typical example.

And thrash Pendil he did, winning by eight lengths after a bravura display of jumping and front-running. Richard Pitman, once again riding Pendil, was left licking his wounds again. There would be a third humiliation in due course.

'In the first King George, I remember lining up on Pendil, who was odds-on, against Christy and I was thinking "dodgy jumper, front runner, I'll let him go". Never saw him again. Never saw him. People think that jockeys are thick and don't think out races beforehand, but of course that's not the case. In that instance I made a real error of judgement there, thinking the horse would fall and I'd be left in front too soon and that Pendil would stop when he was in front,' he remembers.

Pat Murphy maintains, 'That stamped Christy as a true Grade 1 steeplechaser because here was a horse that had won a Sweeps Hurdle, a Scalp Hurdle, he'd been placed in a Champion Hurdle, he won a Gold Cup at his first attempt at the trip and he still retained enough speed to go to Kempton and annihilate the field in the King George – against a classy field. It convinced people in England that this horse was the real deal when his mind was focussed on it. They finally realised he had all the ability under the sun. There are not too many horses since then that could have achieved all those things, are there?'

It was a devastating performance and many were left eating their words – as they would again twelve months later. The truth was that the pre-race hype had annoyed the Samuels and even prompted the mild-mannered Pat Taaffe to issue the following instructions to Bobby Coonan before the race. 'Get out there in front and keep kicking. We'll show the bugger.'

Unfortunately this was a rare gleam of light in what was a terribly wet winter and the ground never really suited Christy's action. He was fourth in each of his next two outings, in the Thyestes at Gowran and the Leopardstown Chase, before dead-heating with Lough Inagh in the PZ Mower Chase at Thurles in his final race prior to defending his Gold Cup crown at Cheltenham.

The festival meeting that year very nearly fell victim to the terrible weather and the first day was cancelled altogether. *Timeform* later declared, 'We'll probably have to wait 'til the next battle of the Somme before we see scenes and conditions similar to those at Cheltenham in 1975.'

Jim Dreaper's Ten Up won that Gold Cup while Christy was pulled up fully a mile from home. He could not cope with the conditions and was unable to pull his feet out of the bog-like ground.

Pat Murphy says that while Christy had already established himself 'among the greats of the game', he does not believe the horse was in the right frame of mind that day.

'When he went to the Gold Cup for the second time he was pulled up at the top of the hill,' he says. 'Yes, it was atrocious ground, but the horse just wasn't up for it. He himself was never up for it. Yes, he was the favourite and yes, he was the reigning champion, but from what I can remember, there was no major confidence in him in the yard going into that Gold Cup. A lot of the reason might have been that we had such a wet, early spring that year.

'The horse did not seem to be sparking the way he had the previous year. Twelve months previously he'd won the PZ Mower in Thurles by a distance, but this time round he only dead-heated with Lough Inagh, and the result had not the same class as his earlier win. The modern-day trainers would have put blinkers on him straight away – I've no doubts about that. The horse had probably got clever at that stage, well, he'd always been clever, but maybe it was he'd gotten cute as well. And I do think (accepting that hindsight is twenty:twenty vision) the modern trainer would have put blinkers on him, although that would probably have blown his brains. And I cannot ever remember Pat considering it even. But looking back from now to 1975, there is no doubt that trainers nowadays would have put blinkers on him. Whether it was that the horse wasn't right or it was the ground that got him, the simple way of putting it is that he did not "fire" on the day. To be honest, he never gave us the feeling going there that he was going to fire. All his preparation had been done on heavy ground – there were no all-weather gallops in those days – and everything was hard work up to the race. The spring was so bad, Ireland was nearly under water and the build-up to the Gold Cup was not smooth at all. Several times we went to do things with the horse and we couldn't because everything was under water – it would not have been safe to do it. That was probably the only time I can remember Pat Taaffe under pressure or seeming to be under pressure. Nothing was clicking into place and everything was a struggle. Looking back on it now – being much older and wiser myself – he was under pressure because of various things not going right. As a professional you have to be under pressure when you have such a high-profile horse. Everyone is asking about the horse and people in this business tend to paint a picture that everything is fine – because that's what you're paid to do.'

Christy won his next race at Naas but was again pulled up in the Irish Grand National, again with a mile to go and again because the ground was bottomless.

What happened next was nothing short of astonishing. The Samuels and Pat Taaffe decided to send Christy to Sandown for the Whitbread Gold Cup, the traditional finale to the National Hunt season. It was undoubtedly a big ask for the horse, but he ran with fantastic guts and determination to finish a gallant second to surprise winner April Seventh, who was carrying a full 2 stone less than the 12 stone Christy was asked to bear.

'He must have been a seriously hardy horse to do all the racing he did,' Tos Taaffe recalls admiringly. 'He was a very good horse and later results like his second in the Whitbread with twelve stone up on him, showed what a horse he was. That was a fair performance, I can tell you.'

The Samuels were not content with that though and they decided to send the horse to France for two engagements the following June. First up was the Prix Du Valais at Enghien near Paris where Bobby Coonan gave Christy a perfect ride, putting him into the lead at the final bend and securing victory over Fair Louis by four lengths.

That was a preparatory run for the Grand Steeple-Chase de Paris at Auteuil on 22 June and everything seemed in place for another victory there. However, the weather was once again to conspire against Christy as it rained heavily in Paris on the day and the already well-watered track became saturated and desperately unsuitable for the Irish horse.

Nevertheless, he was being asked to carry only 10 stone 1 lb over the 4-mile-1-furlong distance and so the conditions did not play as big a part as might have been expected and Christy was once more heroic in his efforts. He went to the front after negotiating the track's 'English ditch' but he did not quite last home, getting beaten by four lengths by the 22/1 outsider, Air Landais.

That autumn, Christy was on the road again, this time to Camden in North Carolina for the Colonial Cup. In truth this was never a race that was going to suit Christy but it was an international race of huge renown with a massive purse and its profile perfectly suited the Samuels' jet-setting image, so he was sent. Pat Taaffe later reckoned that the horse you needed for the Colonial Cup was a one-and-a-half-mile flat horse which had been briskly schooled over hurdles. He schooled Christy himself over the big but flimsy Camden fences, but realised his horse would have to change his jumping style completely if he was to emulate the horses that, American-style, could flick through the low bush-type obstacles that were somewhere in between the hurdles and fences Christy was used to coping with. It was probably an ill-conceived venture, but Christy once more put on a gallant display and actually led three fences from home before being swamped by a host of American horses – Café Prince, Augustus Bay and Soothsayer – before eventually coming home fourth of the eighteen runners.

By now, however, the Samuels' marriage was on the rocks

and, unfortunately, this turn of events would not bode well for Christy or Pat Taaffe for that matter.

One day Jane told Pat that she wanted a divorce, as he relates, 'She was an odd sort of lady. One day she said to me, "You and I are going to get divorced." I said, "Are we? What about our six children?" She said, "You can have three and I'll have three." I said, "Don't be bloody silly, you can't split a family up like that." I said, "I'll tell you what, you can have all the assets I have including Ballinakill and everything that's on it and you look after the six children." So, she did. She was a very funny lady, but she was all right. She'd get in very bad moods at times, but she was very good in raising my children. '

Pat decamped to Australia where he had extensive business interests at the time and he was thus out of the loop when it came to the further adventures of Christy.

While Pat faced incredible difficulties dealing with Jane Samuel in the aftermath of their split, the show still went on and next up for Christy was the Punchestown Chase on 13 December where he convincingly defeated Davy Lad and the previous season's Gold Cup winner, Ten Up. There was plenty of newspaper speculation after the race that, on the back of the performance, Christy now had to be favourite for the 1976 Gold Cup; many commentators also felt that he would not be beaten in the forthcoming renewal of the King George at Kempton, a race he would be attempting to win for the second consecutive year.

Indeed, in his preview of the King George, Michael O'Farrell in *The Irish Times* opined that, on the basis of his Punchestown form, Christy would have the measure of old rival Bula. He was right.

O'Farrell also predicted that Christy would win despite the absence of Bobby Coonan who had been injured in a schooling accident and would be replaced by 21-year-old Gerry Newman.

Tom Taaffe recalls the circumstances. 'Gerry only got the ride in the last couple of days before the race because Bobby Coonan got hurt. Gerry had been riding out with us at the time and my father was happy enough to give him the leg-up. That was my father – once he was happy enough that Gerry was a good enough rider, he was happy with that. He did things his own way. He did that when he was riding and he did that when he was training too. Maybe that's what people didn't like at the end – I'm not sure what way it went.'

Pat Murphy was a little disconcerted that he was overlooked for the ride as he felt he had more experience of the horse than Gerry Newman had, but he accepted the decision and, looking back on it now, says Pat Taaffe was fully vindicated by the victory.

Although nobody knew it at the time, this would be Christy's last racecourse appearance, but what an appearance it was.

He lined up at Kempton on 26 December against six rivals and was sent off as joint favourite with Bula, but none of the opposition saw Christy for dust.

Pat Murphy has vivid memories of the display. 'In the second King George, he had the race won halfway down the back straight, bar a fall and, unfortunately with Christy, you could never rule that out. Gerry was very young, keen and enthusiastic and was only ever looking for a long stride into a fence. But that suited Christy and Gerry gave him a good confident ride and the horse won by a distance. In fact, the horse, probably on that day, was as good as he had ever been in his life, which was quite amazing on the back end of a lot of races. But that was a good King George that day, with a good field and on good ground.

'Yes, he was joint favourite, but he had to put plenty of

disappointments behind him, plus, he had been to America earlier in the autumn for the Colonial Cup. Going there in those days with a horse was a heck of a journey, but the odd thing was – Pat Taaffe reckoned – that the horse actually seemed to thrive on it. And of course he only had the one run at Punchestown before the King George. But, here was a horse that ran in the Colonial Cup on 15 November and literally, under four weeks, later ran at Punchestown and a couple of weeks after that again went to Kempton. That was practically more runs that Best Mate had in a season! Christy did that in three different countries at a time when travel is nothing like as easy as it is now. I remember the whole feeling at the time when he won the second King George that it was as good a performance as we had ever seen from the horse. I was personally delighted for the boss, because he had been under serious pressure. Mrs Samuel was not as good as her husband at taking the defeats. When things went wrong therefore, we all knew about it. But Pat handled it very well and while I could not say there was always a threat hanging over him that the horse could be moved, it was certainly there by times and that was very tough. I had enough about me at the time to realise that that particular victory meant an awful lot.'

It did mean a lot to Pat Taaffe and Christy's thirty-length demolition of the field – he also smashed the track record by four seconds – impressed many others too. *Timeform* described it as 'one of the most exciting exhibitions of galloping and jumping ever seen on a racecourse', while author and commentator Peter Willett said it was 'one of the great performances of steeplechasing history'.

Even at this remove, Tom Taaffe is still awed by what Christy had done in both his King George victories.

'They were epic days,' he says. 'To beat Pendil and Bula were epic days. To beat the two best jumpers of their day – the English talked of both as being in a different league to everything else, much the same way as they talked about Mill House before Arkle came along – was really something. They do get carried away with their own bullshit by times. But I can remember that they simply could not believe what happened in the two King Georges. To beat Bula by two fences and Pendil by nearly a fence was simply incredible. But that was the type of horse he was and hence Kempton was his track.'

Further endorsement, if it is needed, comes from Ted Walsh, who says that he always felt that Christy was an 'aeroplane' and that his achievements still stand him out as special.

'When Captain Christy won the King George he beat Bula by a distance. He jumped out into the lead straight away and the rest of them never saw him again. He had the pace to win a Champion Hurdle – and probably could have won one – and the stamina to win a Gold Cup at three-and-a-quarter miles. Not too many horses can do that. To me the only thing that let him down was the consistency of his jumping. If he could have jumped he would have been – and I've often said this on television – one of the greatest horses of all time.'

The 1975 King George was, sadly, Christy's last public appearance and that fact would have a terrible effect on many of those associated with the horse.

Pat Taaffe had been a little worried about a potential tendon problem since October that year and the following February, as Ivor Herbert would later say, 'the warm niggle became a hot reality'. He had been working Christy on the sands at Portmarnock – the same sands where just a few years previously Bobby had trained horses for Stuart Barrett before deciding on a riding comeback – and he immediately knew the horse was in trouble.

The Irish Times of 11 February 1976 carried a headline

which trumpeted 'Captain Christy is out for rest of season'. In the story under the headline, readers were told that 'Captain Christy, hot favourite for next month's Cheltenham Gold Cup, injured himself at exercise and will not race again this season.'

The story quoted a 'dejected' Pat Taaffe as saying that he had intended to run the horse the following Saturday at Leopardstown, but he had to take him out of the race. 'Although the injury is not a serious one, the knock on his off-fore was severe enough for him to be sidelined for the rest of the season. There is a lot of heat in the leg and the only cure is a long rest,' he told the reporter.

The paper further went on to say that, on veterinary advice, the horse would be rested for six months.

Pat's vet Jimmy Kelly was on hand immediately and he immediately recommended that the tendon be fired★.

'He got a leg at the end of his career and I remember firing him,' Jimmy Kelly says. 'He also had a wind operation which I think might not have been necessary. It was before the era of fibre-optic endoscopes and he might have made a tiny bit of noise, but at that time people regarded a horse which made a noise as a bit of an evil. But a lot of horses make a bit of noise

---

★Firing – or Pin firing as it is more widely known – is, according to American veterinarian Clyde Johnson, a therapy that has become somewhat controversial in modern times, but back in the 1970s it was a commonly accepted way of treating tendon injuries in racehorses. It involves the use of a small, red-hot probe to cause cauterisation (burning) of tissue in horses with chronic injuries to produce an abundant, serous, inflammatory process. As opposed to other inflammation processes such as infections or bruising, serum has little or no fibrin (clotting material) or cellular content and does not coagulate. Firing causes maximal exudation, or oozing, and minimal tissue degeneration. The flooding of serum seems to flush out any chronic irritation, and it does not displace old scar tissue. Firing is done more often in racehorses than in other performance horses, and has been used for more than a century in conditions of recurring injuries such as a splint, curb or chronic bowed tendon. The process is performed under sedation and local anaesthesia, and the pain inflicted is fairly short-lived and usually well-tolerated by the patient.

and it does not affect them at all because the cause of it is not laryngeal paralysis [the causes of which are unknown, or idiopathic, to use the medical term], but some other condition. I think that was a mistake.

'Christy was a very sound horse. But he had made a bit of a noise and he was hobdayed [an operation in which the paralysed bit of the larynx is tied back to prevent it interfering with the horse's breathing]. I don't think he needed it, actually, but he underwent the procedure.'

With regard to the more pressing problem of Christy's injured leg, Jimmy Kelly also recalls that, until that injury occurred, he cannot remember anything else ever going wrong with the horse.

'Most chasers suffer from leg problems at some point, but it didn't happen to Christy until very late,' he says. 'I fired him in Pat's – I remember it well. I really do remember it well because the tranquilisers and analgesics were nothing like as effective as they are now and Christy was not a horse who would take kindly to being interfered with in any shape or form. It was not very difficult really, but we got it done anyway.'

With regard to what was supposed to happen next, Jimmy Kelly has no doubts.

'If you fire a horse or do anything else with them involving their legs, they need twelve months' rest,' he says firmly. 'It's absolutely essential. I still happen to think that firing a horse is the best treatment for tendonitis in horses. If you fire and rest they do better than if they just rest. I have one particular client who, over a very long period of time, kept written records of all the horses I dealt with for him. There is a huge disparity in the results which showed that firing and rest was much better than just rest.'

Jane Samuel was disinclined to believe either Pat Taaffe or

227

Jimmy Kelly and the result had disastrous consequences for the trainer and the horse.

She decided to remove Christy from Pat's care and transferred him instead to Francis Flood's yard. But the horse proved both trainer and vet right and did not stand up to the rigours of training.

'When the horse was taken away,' Jimmy Kelly says, 'Pat would never talk to you about things like that. Maybe he bottled it up, I don't know, or maybe he just moved on. The bottom line – and he knew it – was that Francis would not be able to do any more with the horse than he had. That was how it turned out. But it was a dreadful thing and it would certainly not make you fall in love with Mrs Samuel. The end was very inglorious.'

Jane Samuel took Christy home to Adare where he became unsettled and 'pottery' and so she had him put down.

In technical terms 'pottery' means that Christy was having trouble with his feet, as Jimmy Kelly explains: 'That would suggest he was not getting regular farrier attention. A lot of horses simply cannot be turned out into a paddock with just a New Zealand rug on them; they're not geared for that – certainly not in this damp and wet climate. Former racehorses like to be ridden out and kept active.'

Mrs Samuel's decision to put Christy down was one not many people readily understood, and her by then ex-husband certainly did not.

'Of course I was bloody annoyed,' he says now. 'I was talking to her on the phone and I asked how the horse was and she told me she'd had him put down. She said he had been getting pottery, so she put him down. I told her she had no right to do that as she did not solely own the horse. She said, "Well, I've done it anyway." Obviously I think it was a big mistake, we should have kept the horse alive just because he was so special.

He was still getting a lot of mail when that happened, such was the connection between him and the racing public.

'I asked her what the hell she had done taking the horse away from Pat Taaffe and she replied that she had been to the races somewhere and had asked Pat if Christy would win. He responded that he hoped so and she told him she didn't want a trainer who only hoped. She had got so used to winning that she could never believe he would ever be beaten. She was a wonderful horsewoman herself and had quite a reputation in the horsey world. She was a very strong woman in terms of her opinions and quite bossy. Even though I was a partner in the horse and paid all the bills, she didn't really like me interfering with what she was doing with the horse and she finally had him put down. She never told me anything about it. I had heard he was having leg trouble, but that's all and it was a real shock when I found out he had been put down. I said to her, "Why the hell would you do that?" and she replied, "Well, he's no use any more." I think he deserved better than that.

'Jane was a funny woman in many ways. I have all the trophies and I have the Gold Cup, but she had scratched off the inscription on it which said the owners were "D. W. and J. Samuel". She never entered him in both our names, even though I told her she had to do that. That was probably another reason we got divorced.'

His rueful tone is matched by anyone who ever had anything to do with the horse, Tom Taaffe included. 'It might have been an ignominious end for Christy, but I am not surprised [by Jane's actions]. It was a very sad end for the horse.'

Ted Walsh is even more outspoken. 'When she took the horse off Pat Taaffe, it was regarded by many of the sport's insiders as one of the most disgraceful things ever to have happened.

There was nothing strange about it; she could do anything and she did, usually on a whim.'

Opinions differ as to the effect this had on Pat Taaffe, and Ted Walsh and Pat Murphy have diverse hypotheses.

Pat Murphy maintains that 'it was devastating at the time' for the trainer and caused him to lose his inherent faith in human nature. 'While he never, ever said anything against Jane Samuel – and he even defended her when the horse was taken away – it was hard for Pat.'

Ted Walsh, on the other hand, reckons that it was not terribly heartbreaking for Pat Taaffe 'because the horse was at the end of the road and Pat didn't lose sleep over it. He was leaving as an injured sportsman.'

Whatever the case, it was the end of an era at Alasty. Christy was gone and it would not be long before most of the remaining horses in Pat Taaffe's yard would be gone too.

Joanna's death in 1973 had had a ripple effect on the whole operation. Molly Taaffe had, up to then, looked after all the secretarial duties, but the death of her daughter had a terrible effect on her and consequently most of the business end of the yard was neglected. On top of that, Pat was not a worldly-wise businessman and there were those only too willing to take advantage of the fact.

'My dad was a fantastic horseman and he was not a businessman,' Tom Taaffe says plainly. 'He was a pure natural horseman with a vision for the stride and the vision to ride a race. He was king at that, but take him away from that and he was not a businessman, while some he was dealing with were businessmen and they were well able to take advantage of him and they did so. That was what partly led to his downfall ultimately because he could not handle the pressures of the deals people were forcing him into and hoodwinking him in the process. He was swindled into things. At the same time my mother had her own problems and she was doing the books and as a result the whole thing collapsed. The concrete cracked and everything caved in. That is really where it went wrong. Then, obviously, we lost our sister Joanna which was a major disaster for both parents, because it put my mother off the wall and while my father was strong enough to keep going, it was a period of intense turmoil for him. It was probably lucky they had a great horse to keep them lit up.'

Pat Murphy recalls his time at Alasty as 'probably the best six years of my racing life', but he says the writing was on the wall after Christy was taken away from the yard.

'It was a great time and, looking back now, yes I should have left two years before I did. The operation was going downhill and it was not that I felt I owed Pat anything, but once he was there and the horses were there, then I was going to be there too. He called me in one day to say that Eddie Harty had rung him and wanted me to start riding out. "He wants you to start riding out and I think you should." He was effectively saying to me that it was time I moved on. I did move on and there were no more horses after I went. That was it. I was the last member of staff he had. Very sad when I think back on it.

'Pat Taaffe had many good friends, but he was such a nice man and his only crime in life was that he was probably the worst businessman you've ever seen in your life. People took advantage of that and the worst thing about many of them is that they survived in the racing game and he did not.

'I learned a lot about people there and I learned a lot about honesty because he was a very honest, straightforward and nice man. Far too nice, unfortunately. They were so nice to me, the Taaffes, Pat and Molly, Peter, Carol, Olive and Tom, I just didn't want to leave it. I should have left after four years rather than six, but that was my choice – nobody else's,' he says.

He also maintains that Pat Taaffe's legacy is that he was a born horseman who knew how to deal with horses but not necessarily humans.

'I don't mean the staff by that, because he was always good to his staff. In Captain Christy you had possibly the best steeplechaser that I have come across in my time in the game – and that's a long time now. He had the speed to be placed in a Champion Hurdle and the stamina to win a Gold Cup fifteen months later and still be able to go back and be competitive at two miles after that. The pair of them together was a marriage made in heaven. I really do think that without Pat Taaffe, Christy would never have scaled the heights he did. I genuinely, hand on heart, believe that Bobby, if you like, was the icing on the cake. Bobby was not a stick jockey; he was a tough jockey, but not a stick jockey. His hands and legs and his natural horsemanship made him the perfect partner for the other two. Pat Taaffe never gave you a list of instructions and on the first day Bobby rode Christy, Pat said to him, "Ride him as you find him, Bobby." From that moment on, they were all singing off the same hymn sheet and that was why what happened, happened.

'I think back – God, how lucky was I to work with these people. It is a time I will never regret in my life. There were good and bad times, sure, but to be involved with such gentlemen was fantastic. And, whatever people might say about Bobby, he was a gentleman right to the end. He was one of the great men of racing who hit the highest of the highs and the lowest of the lows and somehow managed to survive and have a life.

'I was there virtually until the end when there were practically no horses left. Pat almost had to force me out of the place. It probably did not do my career any good because I stayed there too long, but I felt safe and secure there. They were a great family, the Taaffes; they really were a great family. And of course, Olive and Tom, Peter and Carol they were all growing up at the same time I was; I was in their age group and got on great with them.'

Tony O'Hehir is adamant that it took a considerable degree of ability for Pat Taaffe to get Christy to do what he did. 'If you take Christy out of the equation, though, I don't think he ever really had another serious horse. Certainly he trained loads of winners, but I don't think he ever had anything like Christy.' Few would disagree.

John Nicholson says there are no two ways about it: Captain Christy was a freak.

'He was a freak because he was not bred to be what he was at all. On his breeding he should not have been what he was. But he was a superstar and he was truly a "people's horse", the same as Arkle was.' That said, he felt for Christy because of what happened. 'It was a very sad ending for a great horse,' he muses.

Pat Murphy is of a similar view and reckons there was nothing in Christy's pedigree and there was nothing in his wider family that had ever shown anything like the class he would show.

'He was a freak of nature and you do get the odd one. One of the greatest flat horses we have ever seen was Mill Reef and he had no pedigree either. He would never have been bought on his breeding. That was one of the great things with Christy – and Pat and the belief he had in him – there was nothing there on paper that told you this was going to be a Gold Cup winner. Not to put too fine a point in it – and looking back over all those years and still no novice has done it since – it took big balls to go and do it. At a time when we had some real, proper Gold Cup horses – they'd all been there and most had done it and were top drawer chasers of their era – and Pat didn't think twice about it. With the incident at the Irish Grand National when he fell and then came out the next day to win the Powers Gold Cup, the thing was that Pat Taaffe knew something could go wrong in the first race, so he entered him in the second one. I'd never personally come across a horse that was mentally like Christy. It is always said of horses that they know when they are good. Christy certainly knew it. He was a bit of a prima donna, but that was because he knew he was good. Maybe it was the way Pat treated him, the way he rode him himself and looked after him – all that sort of thing. But there is no doubt he was a prima donna. He knew damn well the operation was going to centre around him and that was that. He always had this quirky look about him with the ears pricked and the head up a little bit and watching everything that was going on. He decided whether or not anything was for him. It would have been so easy to get it totally wrong.'

Ted Walsh is another to voice the opinion that Christy was a freak. 'The whole pedigree would tell you that,' he maintains. 'The rest of them were useless and there was nothing else ever came out of that family of the same calibre. How does this happen? Who knows? Look at Arkle, for God's sake; what pedigree did he have? None. Desert Orchid was another. But it is much the same for humans as it is for horses. Individuals are brilliant at something and nobody else in the family is any good at it. I'm sure Caruso had brothers who hadn't a note in their heads. Some families are gifted right through, but the real special guys are one-offs. Christy was a genuine one-off.'

Jimmy Kelly is another for whom the word 'freak' springs to mind when Christy is mentioned, but he says he was a brilliant horse who had a great trainer.

'Pat was a smashing man. The term gentleman was coined for him. He was so gentle and yet, with the horses, he was very firm and quite hard. But he was a super person. The bottom line was that he was a good trainer. He was one in a million, in my view. If I had a horse with Pat Taaffe I'd be keeping my fingers crossed it would be able to stand up to the rigours of the training, but knew that if the animal did stand up, he was going to be winning races.'

Whatever about Pat's abilities as a jockey and as a trainer, it was his failure to cope with the financial end of things – the day-to-day boring stuff – which would stop him in his tracks. His son, Tom Taaffe, who followed in his father's footsteps by training a Gold Cup winner (Kicking King in 2005) was very aware of this flaw in his father's make-up. And he was not alone.

Racing journalist and commentator Tony O'Hehir, whose father Micheál was a close friend of Pat Taaffe, says the man was an old-school toff, but one whose innocence of the world at large was quite astonishing. 'Pat Taaffe always struck me as being a little naive. He was a wonderful horseman and a brilliant jockey in his day, but he was never really a man of the world.'

This view is echoed by Jimmy Kelly. 'I was not cogniscent about Pat's affairs, but I do know as a businessman he would not have been as effective as many trainers. He was very bad at sending out bills and I know a couple of people who had horses with him and they might only get a bill every six months. That was not good psychology. But Pat didn't train horses to make money; he trained horses because he loved them and everything to do with them. Down the line, he hoped to make a living, but he was not a dealer or even a wheeler-dealer. He was the epitome of a gentleman.'

Pat Taaffe's last years were spent training point-to-pointers and breaking horses at Alasty. It was not as it should have been, but he also had a serious heart condition and consequently his health was always suspect.

But life went on for him after Captain Christy. The horse last won in December 1975 and Pat Taaffe died in 1992, having some time previously undergone one of the first heart transplant operations in Ireland under the care of Maurice Nelligan.

'Back in 1989 when he was really sick,' Tom Taaffe recalls, 'I had more or less taken over the place and I was stocking it with young horses. I remember driving him to hospital for the operation and I was the family guardian who went to hospital. He was gone one way or another if he did not have the operation and he was waiting for about fourteen months for the right heart. Then I remember a girl was killed in a car crash in Liverpool and her heart came over that night and he was operated on the following day. At the time it was only the third one done here and there was a lot of worry about rejection and so on.

'He had a tough six months immediately after the operation, but after that he had a great eighteen months or so. He was constantly on anti-rejection tablets and the medics were always warning him about the danger of getting any sort of a small cut which could get infected. He had to be so careful – or was supposed to be any way. After a while he wanted to get back riding, which he was not allowed to do, but my mother and myself agreed that he should ride out and he did that most days, pottering around and doing his own thing. He got a great buzz from that. What eventually led to his death was that he was out clipping hedges one day and a thorn pricked him – right into a vein as it turned out. He was a great man for TCP and he washed the thing, but he had gotten an infection into his bloodstream. As a consequence, with the medical people trying to keep the heart from rejecting and also fighting the infection in his blood, he was on some really strong medication and I have to say he had a horrible last couple of months. The drugs were driving him ga-ga, to the point where he thought people were coming in through the walls to get him.

'I used to bring him out to the park most days from where he was in the Mater. But one day I told them I might be a bit longer with him and I took him out here to my place and to the hill where he galloped Christy. I had just bought the place and I was telling him about what I was thinking of doing and he told me that if I could buy this farm I should. I have a certain amount of satisfaction about that – particularly as he had seen it and knew what I was going to do with it. A few days later – and he was not a man of words at all – he told me that he was dying and he wanted to go home to die. He told me the nightmares were having a terrible effect on him and upsetting him greatly. He was crying when he was telling me this.

'At half-past eleven the same night I got a call from the hospital, asking me to come in. When I got there he had passed away. I was so sorry I had not brought him home and in some ways I have never forgiven myself, but it is always very hard to know what the right thing to do is. But if I was ever in that situation again, I'd take the person home – I really would. That was that.

'He was a very passionate man – very quiet and humble, but passionate. To all of us he was a star and he always had time for everyone – any person of any nature. That showed us what a gentleman he was; he always stopped and had a few words with people and he never felt he could walk past people because he was too important to talk to them. That was a lesson he taught us well and for which he deserves our eternal thanks. But he was a very uncomplicated man and unfortunately the world got too complicated for him. It took advantage of him.'

★

And so our story comes to an end.

Captain Christy is still often the subject of bitter pub and racecourse arguments about his jumping abilities; such typically frank exchanges nevertheless always twist at their denouement and consensus emerges, 'yes, but he was some bloody horse'. And he was. In 2004, the *Racing Post* carried out a poll to discover its readers' '100 Favourite Racehorses'. Christy reached number 70 but memories of his greatness may have faded a little by then.

Christy was a genuine freak of nature and he needed special care and attention. He got just that when he came into Pat Taaffe's care and when he was partnered with Bobby Beasley, he found a kindred wild spirit. Between them they confounded convention and ultimately achieved something back in 1974 which has not been repeated since.

Theirs is a unique and maybe even bizarre tale and, as such, it will forever remain part of the folklore of National Hunt racing. It deserves nothing less.

Further Reading

Beasley, Bobby, *Second Start,* W. H. Allen, 1976

Boyne, Sean and O'Neill, Peter, *The Master Of Doninga – The Authorised Biography of Paddy Mullins,* Mainstream, 1995

Clower, Michael, *Kings of the Turf,* Aurum, 2007

Corry, Eoghan, *The Irish at Cheltenham,* Gill & Macmillan, 2009

Green, Reg, *Kings for a Day – Aintree's Bravest Sons,* Mainstream, 2005

Herbert, Ivor and Smyly, Patricia, *Winter Kings: Great Steeplechasers – Lottery to Desert Orchid,* Pelham, 1989

Hopkins, Garth, *Clairtone – The Rise and Fall of a Business Empire,* McClelland and Stewart, 1978

Knight, Henrietta, *Best Mate: Triple Gold,* Highdown, 2004

Lee, Alan, *Fred: the Authorized Biography of Fred Winter,* Pelham, 1991

Rimell, Fred and Rimell, Mercy, *Aintree Iron – the Autobiography of Fred and Mercy Rimell,* W. H. Allen, 1977

Rohmer, Richard, *Golden Phoenix – A Biography of Peter Monk,* Key Porter Books, 1999

Scally, John, *Them and Us: the Irish at Cheltenham,* Mainstream 2000

Smyth, Raymond, *High Rollers of the Turf,* Sporting Books, 1992

Taaffe, Pat, *My Life – and Arkle's,* Stanley Paul, 1972

Tanner, Michael, *The Champion Hurdle,* Mainstream, 2005

Index